MEN AND FEMINISM

Men and Feminism
Copyright © 2009 by Shira Tarrant, PhD

Published by
Seal Press
A Member of Perseus Books Group
1700 Fourth Street
Berkeley, California

10 9 8 7 6 5 4 3 2 1

Library of Congress Cataloging-in-Publication Data

Tarrant, Shira, 1963-
  Men and feminism : Seal studies / Shira Tarrant.
      p. cm.
  Includes index.
  ISBN-13: 978-1-58005-258-0
  ISBN-10: 1-58005-258-4
  1. Feminist theory. 2. Feminists. 3. Male feminists. 4. Sex differences (Psychology) I. Title.
  HQ1190.T376 2009
  305.42081--dc22

                         2008051980

Cover design by Kate Basart, Union Pageworks
Cover illustration © Lauren Simkin Berke c/o rileyillustration.com
Interior design by Michael Walters
Printed in the United States of America by by Maple-Vail
Distributed by Publishers Group West

MEN AND FEMINISM

SHIRA TARRANT, PhD

SEAL
Studies

For Julia Arons, a bright shining star who left us much too soon. And for Kate and Bob Arons. I know you'll carry your sister's memory while you keep making new ones of your own.

Julia Arons
1988–2008

CONTENTS

PROLOGUE

WHAT DO I KNOW ABOUT MEN?

That might be the million-dollar question. I mean, what do any of us know about men, really?

Most of what we think we know about men and masculinity comes to us from movies, music, and ads on TV. We might have heard that men are from one planet and women are from another. (It's not true, by the way.) We learn what it means to be a "real guy" from our friends and families and people in our neighborhoods. Tons of assumptions are out there about biology, testosterone, and manhood that deserve a closer look.

But, still, what do I—as a woman—know about men?

To get at this question, let's just say I did a lot of research. Some of it resulted in my anthology about masculinity and progressive change, *Men Speak Out: Views on Gender, Sex, and Power*. In the process of editing that book, I learned a lot about men's perspectives on a wide range of issues. But I still had many more questions than I did answers. So I spent a lot of time listening and observing. I owe many thanks to all the men I've met along the way who've engaged in conversations and emails about masculinity, who've gone with me to sports bars, porn conventions, and on other adventures, and who've put up with more than a little discomfort from my many, many questions about what they think it means to be a man.

But there's a second part to this book's title: feminism. And that I know lots about. With a PhD in political science and some years under my belt researching and teaching the subject, I found it had come time to take the "men" and the "feminism" and put the two together.

We need it.

As the chapters in this book explain in more detail, so much is to be gained by continuing our conversations about men, masculinity, masculine privilege, and feminism. That's because I believe most men—most *people*—are good. And together we can become even better.

The problem is that we live in a culture that presents us with dominant versions of masculinity as being rough, tough, and rock solid. Men aren't supposed to back down. We are surrounded by images idealizing the bad boy, the bad-ass moneymaker. Or we see TV shows, movies, and advertising that portray guys as irresponsible slackers, perpetual adolescents, bumbling through life with faux-innocent "Who me, get a job?" looks on their faces. Since we're bombarded with these limited selections, it's challenging to think of alternative options for manhood that are appealing and that resonate with who we might want to be, or who we might want to be with.

Personally, I like tough guys. I'll just cop to it front and center. I like smart guys and sensitive ones, too, most definitely. But (to my own peril) I find it easy to fall for those hypermasculine bad-ass guys. (I'm working on it.) All of us make complicated choices about how we live and whom we love. But tough-guy masculinity is only one option that mainstream culture hypes. And narrow options contradict what I know in my head about feminism, which is that it's about maximizing our liberty and minimizing arbitrary constraints based on gender or class, race or sexuality.

Why would I start this book, *Men and Feminism*, with a personal confession about liking bad-ass guys? Because I'm not the only one who feels this way. Plenty of heterosexual men respond to tough masculinity. Gay men, queer women, straight girls do, too. There's a lot of social prodding for it every time we see a movie, go to a football game, pick up a magazine, or watch a political debate. Haven't we been taught our whole lives that the tough guy wins the game? Or, as my student Cassie Comley put it, haven't we always heard that nice guys finish last? Maybe we grew up in families or neighborhoods where being tough seemed to be the only option.

The problem is that being hard is only *one* version of masculinity, and it's a version that's limiting and potentially harmful to men and to the people in their lives.

I cop to my weakness for tough masculinity because I'm as much a part of our culture and the process of critically rethinking it as you, the reader. We all have ways in which our personal lives don't always sync perfectly with our politics, our book knowledge, or our ideals. As humans we are so dang inconsistent. Even downright flawed.

But change and improvement are definitely possible—the kind of change that provides *more* options and freedom.

I invite all of us to join in a delightfully imperfect feminist movement that keeps its eyes on the prize while valuing the process. This process can be as messy and as well intentioned as human beings ourselves. This invitation is for you, whether you're a woman or a man or trans or genderqueer. We're in this together as we try to sort things out to create a more just and equitable world. It is crucial that we start talking with each other across various communities about masculinity and femininity, about gender politics, and about sexuality, race, and class.

The night before I sat down to write this prologue, I moderated a discussion at a screening of the film *Hip-Hop: Beyond Beats and Rhymes*. After we watched the film, I asked the audience what a new vision of masculinity might look like. There was a long silence in the room. Even though we knew in our heads that there are so many possible ways of being men, when it came to describing these out loud, we were all generally stumped. Finally, one guy said he thought being a real man meant having the courage to speak up and to speak one's truth when the time is right.

With *Men and Feminism*, I invite each of us to think more courageously and more deeply about masculinity. I invite each of us to get real about sexuality, power, and gender politics. And then I encourage all of us to speak up when the time is right.

Chapter 1

OVERVIEW AND INTRODUCTIONS: THIS IS WHAT A FEMINIST LOOKS LIKE

BRANDON ARBER IS A FEMINIST. During college, he was the captain of his swim team and an all-around jock. For Brandon, feminism is a moral belief. It's about thinking girls and women shouldn't be raped, abused, discriminated against, or denied health services, especially if they get pregnant. When it comes down to it, he says, feminism is a viable approach to guiding decisions in our personal, political, and public lives. To Brandon, it's just common sense to believe in egalitarian values. It makes sense to care for all people and to bring about a better world.

Greg Bortnichak is a twenty-three-year-old musician who plays in an experimental punk band. Like Brandon, Greg is a feminist, too. Being a male feminist is challenging, Greg explains, because staying true to ideals about equality and justice means he has to consciously pay attention to the way he behaves. Greg first started thinking about gender justice when he was a teenager growing up in what he describes as a "homogeneous New Jersey town." Feminism provided tools for Greg to start thinking critically about gender and race and his unearned privileges as a heterosexual white male. He tries in his everyday life to avoid doing things that oppress other people, and he attempts to confront oppression when he sees it around him. This means, for example, that Greg speaks up and refuses to be complicit when his Starbucks coworkers make racist jokes or talk in sexist ways about women.

1

Derrais Carter graduated from the University of Kansas, where he majored in sociology and African American studies. When Derrais started college, he fell in love with hip-hop and feminism. In fact, hip-hop is what led Derrais to feminist politics when he started thinking about rap lyrics and what he calls "the battlefield of identity." Being a feminist gave Derrais a platform for changing his life and how he understands his relations with others. "I began to see women as more than a video prop, extra, and eye candy," Derrais writes in his essay "This Is What a Feminist Looks Like." Instead he realized that women are highly misrepresented figures in society whom he had been "conditioned to mistreat and ignore." When Derrais taught a group of high school students one summer, the conversation led to culture, capitalism, and globalization. "By understanding feminism," Derrais says, "we were able to talk about how our 'needs' can exploit women in various other countries. The discussion made all of us think more about how we are all connected."

Still, being a male feminist is a rough road, Derrais says. People are full of race- and gender-based assumptions. "As a black male in college, I was often assumed to be on an athletic scholarship," he explains. "And when I wear my 'This Is What a Feminist Looks Like' T-shirt, people have accused me of trying to get laid." Others have said the same about his job at the campus women's center. "I used to get angry about it. Now I see these comments as mere ignorance and a failure to accept that there are men who truly care about women's issues."

Current feminist perspectives are challenging concepts of gender in fresh, new ways. More men are getting involved in feminist movements led by women. And there are plenty of examples of gender activism initiated by men, such as One in Four and Men Can Stop Rape, programs that work to prevent sexual assault. Colleges and universities are increasingly shifting from women's studies to programs that study gender and sexuality more broadly. At the same time, more guys are becoming interested in feminism. As Julie Bindel reports in the *Guardian*, increasing numbers of men are enrolling in courses with feminist content and perspectives.

This book is about men's engagement with feminism historically, about feminism's insights regarding masculinity and masculine privilege, and about men's involvement in feminism today. It's about what men can offer feminism and what feminism can offer men.

What Is Feminism Anyway?

Feminism is a social movement that seeks equality of opportunity for all people, regardless of gender. When there isn't equality of outcome, feminism wants to know why. It is a political perspective that uses gender to critically analyze power—who has it, who doesn't, who abuses it, and why. In their anthology, *The Fire This Time: Young Activists and the New Feminism*, Vivien Labaton and Dawn Lundy Martin define contemporary feminism as a way for women and men to do "social justice work while using a gender lens."

Feminists are committed to addressing problems that happen every day. Some of these issues take place behind the privacy of closed doors; others confront us in the public arena. These problems include things such as domestic violence, rape and sexual assault, racism, homophobia, unequal pay, job segregation, sexual objectification, restrictions on reproductive choices, and unattainable standards of gender, beauty, and behavior. In her article "Can Men Be the Allies of Feminism?" journalist Nighat Gandhi describes feminism as "a philosophy and a movement for ending all forms of oppression, including gender-based oppression."

On an individual level, feminism seeks to make room for all of us to explore who we are, separate from gender constraints. Too often, the social rules and regulations for men and women are restrictive. They don't really describe us well. Feminism questions rigid binary categories of masculinity and femininity, looks at the political consequences of assumptions about gender, and helps us search for better models and greater freedom.

Three core theoretical principles are especially important to understanding what feminism is about. These principles, which involve specific approaches to analyzing social and political issues,

What Does Feminism Mean to You?

To me, feminism is about balance and equality. I think men feel threat-ened by feminism, yet they should embrace that balance. The feminist movement is the first stone that will make ripples in the water. I call myself a feminist because I grew up surrounded by my sisters and my mom.

—Randy Hoang, twenty-six-year-old computer technician

I guess I'm a feminist because I believe that women are equal to men intellectually. But don't I have to be a woman to be a feminist?

—Anthony K., twenty-three-year-old government employee

Feminism means that women should have the same rights in the eco-nomic, social, and political arena as those of men. I suppose I'm a femi-nist because I believe that everyone—regardless of gender—should have the same opportunities. Opportunity should be open to all and based on qualifications, not gender. I recommend that men should be respectful, mindful, and open to the idea.

—anonymous thirty-four-year-old civil service worker

To me, feminism is the attempt to end subjugation of others based solely on an aspect of their identity, such as culture, race, gender, sexual ori-entation, or class. Although I agree with these goals, I do not call myself a feminist because I believe that, unfortunately, this term is very polar-izing and often creates an oppositional atmosphere.

One of the crucial goals of feminism today needs to be a redefinition of its aims. I think that many people view feminism as an inversion of current oppressive systems, or nothing more than an effort to replace a patriarchal system with a matriarchal one. Instead, I think it's beneficial *to articulate the purpose of feminism as a critique of current power structures and striving for equality, rather than replacing one oppressive system with another.*

—Jason Giffard, twenty-seven-year-old graduate student

Feminism is the belief in equality between the sexes and the struggle to attain it. That struggle is daunting since we live in a world dominated by Caucasian males blinded by the allure of The Almighty Dollar. I truly believe economics is the core issue when it comes to race and gender.

Though I catch hell from most of my male peers, I do consider myself a feminist because I'm aware of the inequalities that exist and I do my best to inform and make change when and where I can. I love people and the best way I can reflect that love is to try to make the world a better place.

I don't see many men caring about feminism. And when they do, it's more passive. Almost as if they are embarrassed by their feelings. Male passivity is one of the biggest problems the feminist movement faces.

—Brian, thirty-two-year-old skater/painter/writer

Feminism means supporting men who take on active parenting roles or who are working to end male violence or who are fighting sexism and homophobia. Men can be feminists just as much as women can. And I think that most men these days actually are feminists at heart but may not ever have thought about the issues directly. Since feminism is all about creating gender acceptance, it's not necessarily a female thing. Feminism is just as much about thinking about how we understand masculinity as it is about defining femininity.

—Matt Gribble, twenty-one-year-old student

I don't call myself a feminist, but I support people who dedicate themselves to feminism, and I try to treat all people equally.

—Christopher Schivley, twenty-nine-year-old police officer

also point to why feminism isn't just a movement for women. Gender and power are crucial elements in all people's lives. First, feminists do not see biological sex as determining a person's identity. Second, feminism understands that the personal is political. Yet feminism is not *only* personal. It's more than a lifestyle issue or a fashion statement or a strategically placed political tattoo. This points to the third core principle: Feminism is a social and political movement that is concerned about the patterns of domination and the politics of gender, race, class, and sexual orientation.

Biology Is Not Destiny

A central core of feminism is the idea that our biological sex doesn't determine our life goals, emotions, behaviors, and preferences, and it shouldn't determine our opportunities. To convey this idea, innumerable feminist thinkers—Simone de Beauvoir, Ann Oakley, and Christine Delphy among them—have challenged the concept of biological determinism and emphasized the distinction between sex and gender.

"Sex" basically refers to our biology—what's between our legs when we're born. Gender refers to our social class as men and women or—when we don't fit into either of these categories—as transgender or genderqueer. Gender is something that is fluid and learned: We might come into this world with a penis or vagina, but we're not born wanting to fix things with a hammer or carry a purse. We learn gender-appropriate behavior as we go along—or we don't, and we might suffer for it. Gender is taught and reinforced through institutional arrangements that tell us how men and women "should" behave. In other words, gender is about the social construction of masculine, feminine, or genderqueer identity. Gender is not a binary selection but, rather, a continuum of possibilities.

Gender isn't something we're born with. It's something we perform. And we learn about *doing* gender through friends, school, religion, and family. We are taught to "do" our gender in many ways.

Our parents might tell us to toughen up when we go out for

sports. If we're boys, our parents might not worry if we stay out late. If we're girls, we might get in trouble for getting angry. For birthday presents we might get Bratz dolls or skateboards, action figures or video games. Chances are that games with action-adventure names such as *Rogue Trooper* or *Call of Duty* are going to the boys. Even toys for the imagination and upping the smarts are often gender coded. LeapFrog, for example, is a toy that teaches kids vocabulary. Yet the cartridges have gender-based names such as "Disney Princess Stories" and "Thomas the Really Useful Engine." The recommended age for these toys is under ten.

Pop culture is another powerful way that gender is constructed, reinforced, and maintained. Pop culture is a potent institutional source of gender messages because we're exposed to it pretty much all day, every day. Every time we log on to the Internet, surf TV channels, watch YouTube clips, go to the movies, or pass a billboard on the side of the road, we are getting messages about masculinity and femininity, how to do it "correctly," and what happens if we don't.

Take Facebook, MySpace, myYearbook, or whatever the flavor of the day. Social networking sites are full of gender lessons. What this means is that some people might post pics to their sites flashing lots of cleavage. And some might not. It's not that *all* women show skin and *no* men ever do, but for the most part, who does it and who doesn't breaks down along masculine and feminine gender lines.

It's hard to find a MySpace photo of a guy sprawled across his bed in tiny lace panties, coyly licking his lips, but this type of image is ubiquitous among young women. These poses take their cues directly from mainstream pornography, which increasingly infuses our everyday lives and models for gender and relationships. We might want to pay attention to who's wailing the heavy metal and who's uploading sloshy love songs to their sites. Are people using "boy" colors and "girl" colors for the backgrounds on their homepages? These sorts of everyday experiences help create and reinforce our gender—and our sexual—identities. Often we participate in this process without really thinking about it.

Even Internet spam is gendered, with proposals by women to

send nude pics and offers to men for penile enhancement products that promise hardness, lasting power, and bigger size. These adjectives construct gendered ideas about masculinity as being strong, hard, and "built." Even what seem to be innocuous ads are actually loaded with gender cues. Take, for example, a 2008 *Martha Stewart Living* magazine ad for grilling spices. The photo shows a man standing over the barbecue with his arms raised high over his head in victory, while the ad copy reads: "Master the Flame. Master the Flavor." Messages such as these create images of the male body as functional, triumphant, in charge. Not that there's anything inherently wrong with these qualities. But because we are so relentlessly bombarded by this limited vision of masculinity through jokes, media, consumer products, and souped-up science that masks underlying politics, these gender messages start to seem normal or "just the way things are." Sometimes we hardly even notice the process, and gender messages become naturalized. In other words, we see gendered messages so often that what are in fact constructed ideologies come to seem natural or essential. Feminism provides critical tools and analytical frameworks that help us notice and that make visible the coded metaphors of gender and sexuality.

With all the pressures of early and ongoing gender socialization, it's no wonder that by the time we're grown up, most nurses, strippers, and kindergarten teachers are still women and most politicians, professors, and firefighters are still men; most stay-at-home parents are women and most CEOs are men; most people with eating disorders are women and most people who use performance-enhancing drugs are men. Gender expectations and assumptions affect all of us—not just women. Fortunately, it looks as if change is on the horizon. We're in the middle of some shifting times when it comes to gender roles and expectations of masculinity and femininity. For now, though, there's still much work to be done.

The Personal Is Political

"The personal is political" is a powerful slogan that was coined during the women's movement of the 1960s and 1970s. It means that what happens in our individual, private lives—at places such as our jobs, clubs, homes, or schools—reflects the power dynamics in broader, public society. As the twentieth-century political scientist Harold Lasswell famously said, politics is the process of who gets what, when, and how. Feminism brings that concept from the public realm into our personal worlds. It recognizes that seemingly personal issues point to larger, institutionalized practices and are therefore legitimately political issues.

Another way to understand this concept is to ask questions such as who gets the goods and resources in society and who bears the burdens? Who sits in positions of power in Fortune 500 companies and who cleans the company offices? Who does the bulk of parenting and who gets paid more on the job? Who is sexually bought and who buys sexual access to bodies? Who is statistically more likely to experience domestic violence and who are the violent offenders? Who gets catcalled on the street? And while we're at it, we can ask who risks their lives in war. Who makes the decisions to go to war in the first place?

These questions point to complicated political and social issues that matter to each of us at the end of the day in deeply personal ways. When we're sitting at home and just want to chill, and we're wondering who's going to watch the kids, or when we're counting how much cash we have to make it until payday, we can look to feminism to help us critically assess the gendered aspects of these experiences.

Gender roles are shifting a bit. But across the board, men still earn about 25 percent more money than women (before we account for race). According to information collected by the U.S. Census Bureau, men spend 50 percent less time grocery shopping than women do. Although men are doing more housework than they used to do, women still shoulder the bulk of it. Diane Swanbrow, of the University of Michigan Institute for Social Research, reports that these days American men do about sixteen hours of housework each week—an increase from the twelve hours a week they did in 1965, but much less than the twenty-seven hours women are clocking each week.

A man's work is never done...

Cartoon by Nicholson from The Australian

Although gender roles in the home are changing, men still do far less housework than women.

Violence is another gendered aspect of our personal lives. While men and boys make up about 10 percent of victims in all reported rape cases, men are the perpetrators in more than 90 percent of all sexual assaults and all violent crimes. According to the FBI and the U.S. Department of Justice, nearly 99 percent of the offenders in single-victim sexual-assault cases are male and these perpetrators are most likely to be white.

Of course, this doesn't mean that more than 90 percent of all men are rapists. And we know that women can commit violent crime as well. What this does mean is that according to current evidence, the vast majority of violence against women (and other men) is perpetrated by men.

This reality connects directly back to the idea that the personal is political. Rape is something that happens to individual women, and it is incredibly personal. Because the risk of sexual assault is far greater for women than for men, this risk keeps many women fearful, restricting their access to some spaces. Rape is sometimes used as a threat or a menacing "joke" toward women who are perceived to be pushing for too much. Rape is something that individual men commit, yet it is supported on a societal level by a culture that encourages men to prove their worth through their physical strength and their sexual power.

During the past several centuries of the women's rights movement, feminism (whether or not it was called by that name at the time) gave women a tool to examine their daily lives to determine how society's sexism was affecting them on a personal level. Women and girls are still asking these questions—and men can, too. It matters who washes the dishes, who takes out the trash, who feels safe walking down the street, and who gets a raise at work. These are political issues. It's all about who gets what, when, and how. Or who doesn't.

Guys have lots of opportunities to examine and make change in everyday issues such as coparenting, pay equity, and consensual sex. Changing diapers might not seem a political act, but it definitely has political meaning. There's certainly nothing wrong with doing domestic, caring work. In fact, feminism is about the right to freely choose our life activities. But if women are doing the majority of the housework and caring for the babies, it means they're doing these unpaid jobs *in addition* to other paid work or it means they're *not* doing something else (such as earning money, writing the great novel, etc.). Warren Farrell, a writer on men's issues, explains that trying to change women's roles ultimately gets stalled if men's roles don't also change. "For example, moms can't break glass ceilings unless dads are caring for the children," Farrell writes in *Does Feminism Discriminate Against Men?* (Farrell was formerly a board member of the National Organization for Women, yet today he controversially argues that men are the victims of discrimination by feminism.)

Feminism not only resists assumptions that women's place is in the kitchen, but it also questions why only young men have to register for the military draft. It prods us to think about inequity and also about the ways in which institutional and legal structures reinforce binary ideas about gender that try to shove all of us in identity boxes that don't necessarily fit and don't always define us well.

Here's an everyday example of how the personal can be deeply political and how feminism helps us think through our actions. (Some of the details in this story are changed to protect people's identities.) Recently, two students were chilling on the grass of their college campus. One of them was a young male student wearing a black T-shirt that said CHERRY BUST 2008 across the front in large white letters. Let's call this guy Cherry Bust Boy. Nearby was another male student who was reading a book on geology. We'll call him Geology Guy. They were both studying for class, the wires from their MP3 earbuds hanging down across their chests. When Geology Guy looked up and saw the Cherry Bust T-shirt, a mixed look of curiosity and concern registered on his face. He turned to Cherry Bust Boy and started talking to him. Here's how the conversation went:

> Geology Guy: *So tell me about your shirt.*
> Cherry Bust Boy: *It's just about a party. It's just the name of a party.*
> GG: *Just? Really?*
> CBB: *Yeah, it doesn't mean anything.*
> GG: *It doesn't mean anything? Are you kidding? Of course it means something. Think about it. There's a lot going on there. Cherry Bust isn't just a shirt. It's not only a party. It's about taking a girl's virginity. And we're not talking consensual sex here. That's not the innuendo. Let's be real. If your T-shirt said* LYNCHING PARTY *2008, would it be just a T-shirt?*
> CBB: [slowly zipping up sweatshirt to cover T-shirt] *What do you want me to do? Take off my shirt?*
> GG: *That's up to you. You have free-speech rights. So do I. And I'm just saying that you ought to think about it. This is personal, but it's not only about you. There's a lot more going on here than just one guy wearing one T-shirt.*

This guy's decision to wear the Cherry Bust T-shirt sent a strong political message reinforcing a focus on women as sexualized bodies that men have a right to access. Wearing the shirt was required by the fraternity he was pledging, so this encounter really speaks to larger cultural issues on campuses nationwide. This example also points to how the personal can be political in positive, progressive ways as well. This conversation was personal (or interpersonal), and it was also profoundly political because it questioned out loud some assumptions about sexuality, gender, and power.

The idea that the personal is political can be a tool to help us explore prevailing ideas about what it means to be a man or a woman in our society and how we internalize these ideas. Understanding how power and domination are both personal and political can also help us incorporate class, race, ethnicity, ability, age, sexuality, religion, and nation of origin—as well as gender—into the feminist equation.

Feminism Is a Social and Political Movement

Feminism is a social and political movement with the goal of ending women's subordination. But it doesn't stop there. The category of woman is amazingly varied, and different women experience gender and gender oppression in different ways depending on class, race, sexual orientation, and more. It's necessary to understand how gender, race, ethnicity, and class are not separate systems of oppression, writes legal scholar Patricia Hill Collins in the journal of feminist philosophy, *Hypatia*. These systems interact with each other and shape how a person experiences power or oppression.

The term "intersectionality" was introduced by black feminists who argued that white feminists who ignored the interaction of race and gender systems obscured problems uniquely faced by women of color. More to the point, writes political scientist S. L. Weldon, "Black feminists argued that their problems and experiences could not be described as the problems of Black men plus the problems of white women. Black women face many problems as Black women, and their unique perspectives, identities and experiences cannot be derived from examination of the experiences and position of either Black men or white women."

Intersectionality introduces critical perspectives on the complex interrelations of gender, race, class, and sexuality. Feminist theorist bell hooks frames this concept in terms of margin and center; author Gloria Anzaldúa describes experiences as "border" or *mestiza* consciousness; legal scholar Kimberlé Crenshaw uses the term "intersectionality theory." To make a difference, intersectional analysis must go beyond describing individuals' identities. This framework enables us to use a feminist lens for understanding transnational issues such as imperialism, pollution, war, human trafficking, and globalization. Intersectional analysis can be used to work toward the systemic change needed for all people to be able to maximize participation in free societies.

Robert Jensen, author of the antiporn book *Getting Off: Pornography and the End of Masculinity*, also points out that intersectional analysis can help us understand men's lives as well as women's. He argues that living in patriarchal cultures where male domination is the norm doesn't mean that all men have it easy. "Other systems of dominance and oppression," Jensen writes, such as "white supremacy, heterosexism, predatory corporate capitalism—mean that non-white men, gay men, poor and working-class men suffer in various ways. A feminist analysis doesn't preclude us from understanding those problems but in fact helps us see them more clearly."

In a video about her work on cultural criticism and transformation, bell hooks explains that the real issue in feminism is not men or masculinity, *per se*, but instead patterns of domination. Abuses of power and the constellation of ways they take shape must have our attention, she argues, if we are to be successful in our struggle for collective liberation. What hooks means is that people may experience exploitation as isolated individuals, but to make change we must recognize the structural patterns that replay over and over and affect people in systemic ways. For hooks, social, political, cultural, and economic oppression is based on repeating patterns of "white supremacist, capitalist patriarchy"; she calls this the politics of domination.

The problem isn't men, but men *are* part of the problem. And no matter our gender, we need to be willing to confront the ways in which men participate in systems of domination (while also understanding that feminism isn't about hating men). Otherwise, it's like having conversations about racism without wanting to talk about the ways in which individual white people enact racism. Or it's like saying "gay bashing is bad" without calling out homophobes for their violence.

Feminism's commitment to social and political transformation means making major social, economic, political, and cultural changes in our society. This commitment can take many forms—working for better legislation, breaking glass ceilings in the business world, supporting battered women's shelters, refusing to collude in racist or sexist jokes, or promoting gender equity in pop culture. Making change also means we all have to examine our own place in various systems of domination—how we benefit and how we're held back. Ultimately, feminism is about making a positive difference and being willing to do the hard work of figuring out what this change might look like.

There's Room for Men

One question that often comes up is how feminism is relevant to men. If feminism is a women's movement, then where do men fit in?

The idea that only women can be feminists is based on essentialism—the assumption that men and women possess inherent behavioral traits based on biological sex. Sometimes people think the term "feminist men" is an oxymoron, says sociologist Michael Kimmel. In his essay "Who's Afraid of Men Doing Feminism?" Kimmel explains that essentialism leads us to think that a feminist man is either not a "real" man or he cannot be a real feminist.

But just as being a woman doesn't make someone a feminist, being a man doesn't automatically mean he's not one. The "feminist-equals-woman" equation is a dangerous way of thinking, explains Judith Grant, author of *Fundamental Feminism*. That perspective blurs the point that feminism is about the interpretive lens we're using, not women's experience as women. Anyway, not all women are the same, just like all men aren't the same. Our gender position is always affected by our socioeconomic, racial, national, sexual, and religious identities.

"Feminism is a political way of thinking," explains Matthew Shepherd in "Feminism, Men, and the Study of Masculinity." "And, like all political thought," Shepherd writes, the attractions of feminism "cut across sex." Being a feminist doesn't require certain plumbing. It requires a certain consciousness. Feminism is about using a particular lens that filters how we understand the world. This lens is analytical and always puts gender front and center. Feminists don't necessarily

You Don't Have to Be Female to Be a Feminist

At times it might seem that feminism is something only women do—or that it's something only women *should* do. It's not uncommon for domestic violence shelters or rape crisis hotlines, for example, to bar men from volunteering with women. There are compelling arguments for single-sex organizing, for instance the concern that men's presence may be traumatizing for women who have been recently hurt by men. This fear is legitimate and important. Women-only groups can also play important roles in providing opportunities for women to develop strategies of survival and resistance. Single-sex groups can support women in exploring anger, fear, internalized sexism, and collusion with their own subjugation, giving voice to these issues that matter so deeply.

But there are ways that men can respect the need for some women-only spaces and still get involved in feminist issues. Men work alongside women in feminist groups advocating reproductive freedom. Some feminist issues, such as male violence against women, sexual harassment, and employment inequities, are most effectively solved by stopping the problems before they happen. And men have a central role in preventing physical, emotional, and economic violence.

Single-sex feminist groups for men can help men process, organize,

think that men and women are the same. Instead, they question the assumptions that biology is destiny and that might makes right. Feminists ask why difference comes at such a high price.

Essentialism also reinforces the binary idea that there are only two, opposite genders; in doing so, it limits our understanding of gender politics. Thinking of feminist-as-female excludes transgender, genderqueer, and intersex people, which is inconsistent with the principles of gender justice. According to activist and scholar Susan Stryker, the rise of queer and transgender studies has challenged essentialist-based politics. In her essay "(De)Subjugated Knowledge," Stryker writes that trans studies calls for "new analyses, new strategies and practices, for combating discrimination and injustice based on gender inequality." If we think of feminism as something that and take action. A few examples include the National Organization for Men Against Sexism, the White Ribbon Campaign, which works to end male violence against women, and various men's support programs organized through the Men's Resource Center for Change in Amherst, Massachusetts.

At the same time, single-sex groups are exclusionary and don't serve the needs of genderqueer and transgender people who may not strictly identify as male or female or who may be rejected by single-sex groups. (Such exclusion has been the source of ongoing controversy at the Michigan Womyn's Music Festival, for example, where a woman-born-woman-only policy means that transwomen who were born male are denied entry.)

As with any kind of effective political action, feminism requires coalition building, strategizing, and talking with others who may not always share our perspectives or understand our experience firsthand. That means thinking seriously about men's role in feminism.

Feminism is an inclusive social movement. It's about taking action in the interest of women and also on behalf of all groups that are affected by hegemonic power. Thinking of feminism as a girls-only club would make feminism a political movement with inclusive goals but with exclusive membership. And that doesn't quite make sense.

women do or believe in, then we conflate feminism with women. This essentializes a political perspective while paradoxically arguing against essentialist foundations.

Feminism benefits from men's participation. When men are involved in gender justice efforts, it maximizes the potential for deep, sustained social change. One practical advantage is that there is strength in numbers and feminism could use more allies. Plus, for the moment, as violence-prevention expert Jackson Katz suggests, men can be heard in ways that women still can't be heard. "Sexist?" Katz asks rhetorically. "Maybe. But effective? Yes."

Men's participation in feminism is not an invitation for male chivalry or for "protecting our women." A protectionist model actually perpetuates the gender stereotypes that are part of the problem, not part of the solution. Getting men involved with feminism means holding men personally and institutionally accountable for the sexist abuse of power, explains Katz. We need more men to challenge other men's sexism or misogyny as it manifests in all sorts of ways. Katz challenges men to move beyond defensive posturing and be willing to call it like it is.

Once again, bell hooks is instructive in discussing men's role in feminism. She writes in *Feminist Theory: From Margin to Center* that men are women's "comrades in struggle." Defining feminism as a movement "to end sexist oppression enables women and men, girls and boys, to participate equally in revolutionary struggle. . . . Men who actively struggle against sexism have a place in feminist movement. They are our comrades."

Joining the Struggle

When punk-rock feminist Chris Crass was hanging out with anarchist political groups in Southern California, his commitment to gender justice went hand in hand with opposing war, feeding homeless people through Food Not Bombs, and supporting students' rights. Chris recognized that ending sexism is key to radical change both within political movements and throughout broader society. For Chris, this continues to mean working with women and men as "allies to each other in the struggle to develop models of anti-racist, class-conscious, pro-queer, feminist manhood that challenges strict binary gender roles and categories." For Grantlin Schafer, being a "comrade in struggle" means working to prevent male violence through his job as an antiviolence educator for a sexual and domestic violence center in Loudoun County, Virginia. These men provide just two examples of the myriad ways men can get involved in feminism.

Nighat Gandhi explains that feminism is about transforming institutions such as the law, the family, the workplace, or marriage to weed out their injustices. Feminists don't necessarily want to destroy these institutions and practices. Many feminists simply want to see them changed into more equitable situations. Men are not excluded from these efforts. In fact, Gandhi says, men should very much feel a part of feminism.

Jackson Katz points out that Americans like to brag how we're "the freest country on earth," yet half of us don't even feel free enough to walk by ourselves at night. Many women aren't even safe in their own homes. By conservative estimates, 20 percent of adolescent girls have been physically or sexually assaulted by a dating partner. Two-thirds of American men responding to a major American public opinion poll in 2000 said that domestic violence is very or fairly common. And 92 percent of people who answered a 2005 national survey said that "family violence is a much bigger problem than people think." And these issues are not unique to the United States.

As Katz points out, it's a mistake to think of sexual assault or domestic violence as "women's issues." Men's violence against women is really more about men than it is about women, Katz explains in *The Macho Paradox: Why Some Men Hurt Women and How All Men Can Help.* What he means is that because men are the "ones committing the vast majority of the violence," it's time for men to face up and do something about it. We live our lives *in relation* to other people, Katz notes. Something that affects women no doubt affects men—and vice versa.

As we'll explore in more detail later in this book, when it comes to issues such as pay inequity or male violence toward women, there's a tremendous amount of work that men can do to stop the problem *before* it even happens! Prevention is

The group Men Can Stop Rape takes on sexual assault as a men's issue. The slogan "Our Strength Is Not for Hurting" encourages men to practice consent in their sexual relations and to rethink what masculine strength is all about.

the real solution. The most important thing is that we talk with each other as we continue coalition building between women and men and across the political spectrum.

Justice Is a Renewable Resource

Some men steer clear of feminism because they have been taught that it's a movement to take power, resources, authority, and perks from men. The real issue is *not* what men might lose: All of us—women and men alike—actually have a lot to gain from feminism. The problem is that power is often seen as a limited resource. This view of power assumes that if one group gains power, another loses it. Or that if one person achieves resources, it must necessarily happen at someone else's expense.

This scarcity model assumes that there are limited resources in the world and that if I get mine, you can't have yours. For those accustomed to this kind of thinking, the assumption is that if women gain power, men will necessarily lose it. But instead of thinking that equality and justice are finite resources (like fossil fuels), there are other ways to view it. If our power grid is fueled by wind or sun, one person's increase in power doesn't mean that there's less to go around. It is possible that we can work cooperatively toward achieving egalitarian conditions. It is possible to think of power as an infinite resource that won't run out when we challenge harmful or limiting gender expectations.

Feminism is about breaking down gender expectations that limit everyone. Feminism holds the potential for each of us to experience a fuller range of possibilities to exist freely in the world and to explore our full humanity while minimizing or eradicating oppression, subjugation, and patterns of domination.

Although equality and gender justice are unlimited resources, feminism does challenge men to change their behavior and to change systems from which they benefit. This requires hard work that some men resist—relinquishing some of the privileges that come with being a man, rethinking sexual pleasure that relies on a woman's denigration, and surrendering unearned authority.

Feminism is a movement for ending gender-based oppression and all forms of related patterns of domination and subjugation in our homes, our communities, and the world. There is a serious and growing movement of men who stand beside women in tackling issues of gender, race, class, sexuality—as well as enormous, complex problems such as war, imperialism, and globalization. These issues are all part of the same package and feminism can be used to address each of them, and more. Sociopolitical issues as seemingly diverse as sexual harassment and the war in Iraq are linked by similar patterns of domination, in which people or groups attempt to obtain power over others. Feminism can offer a new vision of shared power.

Who Me? A Feminist?

Sometimes guys don't get involved with feminist politics because they don't feel welcome. Even walking into a women's studies classroom for the first time can be a challenging experience. Men frequently don't engage with feminism because they think the issues don't involve them. They just can't relate. Or it never occurred to them to get involved in the first place. Not because they're bad men. Maybe it just never crossed their minds.

At the same time, feminist groups that are made up largely of women may intentionally or inadvertently exclude men. Cliques happen anywhere. Politics is no exception. Even social justice and gender politics. It happens. We won't pretend it doesn't.

Men might sometimes feel intimidated by feminism. Or they can believe (or presume) that they are unwelcome to join activist groups. It might feel uncomfortable or strange to stand in a bookstore looking at the feminist titles on the shelves. And sometimes stereotypes about feminists act as barriers that impede men's (and women's) participation.

Stereotypes are a way of labeling people and sticking them in pigeonholes. Stereotypes can be based on a person's race, gender, hair color, sexuality—or even political views. The Guerrilla Girls describe stereotypes as a box that people get jammed into. This box is usually too small to really describe someone.

Is It Really That Funny?

There are many stereotypes about feminists and feminism. Some are framed as jokes such as the following:

Question: *How many feminists does it take to change a lightbulb?*
Answer: *That's not funny.*

Jokes are powerful because they can—as in this example—mask aggression with humor. Being funny makes this aggression invisible. One way to understand antifeminist jokes (or, similarly, jokes that hypersexualize women) is to look at the *effect* of the joke if not the *intent* of the person telling it.

When people object to antifeminist or sexist jokes, they risk being ridiculed or dismissed as humorless. What's really going on here is that jokes become an indirect form of intimidation. The implicit message is that if you aren't willing to go along with the banter, there must be something wrong with you. This process reinforces the bonds among those in the "in group" by ostracizing others. In the case of antifeminist or sexist jokes, the effect is to reinforce men's power and women's subjugation. In "The Fraternal Bond as a Joking Relationship," author Peter Lyman explains that antifeminist or "sexist jokes must be analyzed as mechanisms by which the order of gender domination is sustained in everyday life." Sexist jokes are often used to support male bonding, but such bonding comes at the expense of women, Lyman writes. Understanding this process is an important key in decoding gender, humor, and sexism to reveal the mechanisms of power and masculinity.

Stereotypes can take the form of accusatory or dismissive generalizations. These might include sweeping, silly characterizations, such as the notion that all feminists are angry women with hairy legs who burn their bras or don't wear makeup. Other stereotypes are more blatantly hostile, such as calling a feminist a male basher. "Feminazi" is a particularly pernicious stereotype popularized by the reactionary, right-wing media figure Rush Limbaugh. Jackson Katz points out how using this term is effective in silencing people. After all, who wants to be called a Nazi? And what's more, the term is absurd. This word melds "feminism"—a political effort in part concerned with ending male violence—with "Nazi"—a hypermasculinist movement obsessed with male power over women and the genocidal embodiment of violence.

Obviously, stereotypes can hurt. They can limit our sense of self and our belief in what we're capable of doing and achieving. Stereotypes can be really dangerous, especially when people treat us according to their simplified ideas about us. But stereotypes about feminists are also powerful ways of diminishing the strength of a political movement. Nobody likes to be called a wimp or a man-hating dyke. And, no: If a guy says he's a feminist, it doesn't mean he's lying, whipped, or trying to get with a girl. Those are stereotypes, too. Another misperception—assuming that male feminists are gay—melds political preference with sexual orientation and promotes stereotypes about masculinity, sexuality, politics, and feminism.

Stereotypes about feminism have real consequences. If we don't want to be associated with feminism, we risk distancing ourselves from an important source for understanding our lives and for changing inequitable social, economic, and political realities. If we are silenced by stereotypes or jokes, then we aren't standing up to violence and the abuse of power.

Do I Have to Call Myself One?

What's in a name? Does it matter if you call yourself a feminist, a pro-feminist, a feminist ally, or even a member of the Men's Auxiliary? What if you practice your politics and don't want to label yourself?

Debates over terminology are nothing new—and they aren't limited to men. In the 1940s and '50s, for example, there were those who promoted women's rights and who objected to oppressions of all sorts, but who distanced themselves from the term "feminist." Back then there were all sorts of reasons some people shied away from the label. To call oneself a feminist risked evoking images of being militant, racist, a sexual prude, bourgeois, strident, or just plain selfish. Similar assumptions are still made today. Both men *and* women who identify as feminists risk being called what historian Leila Rupp refers to as manhaters and crazies, kooks or queers.

Because there is concern that feminism focuses primarily on white women's issues and uncritically assumes white experience as the norm, some shy away from the term "feminist" because it doesn't go far enough. Thinkers and activists have developed terminology and frameworks to intentionally reflect the matrix of race, class, gender, and ethnicity. Womanism, for example, focuses on how black women experience power, oppression, and status within the social hierarchy. Womanism uses this concept as a base for advocating social change and improved gender politics by providing an option for social and political analysis that makes black women and other women of color central. Similarly, black feminism, *mujerista* theology, and woman of color feminism are all approaches to sociopolitical transformation. Although none of these is a subset of feminism, each uses similar tools of political analysis and shares a commitment to confront sexism.

Some men who recognize these problems of gender repression, misogyny, sexism, and the politics of domination take a stand by identifying as feminists. Others call themselves pro-feminists, feminist allies, antisexist activists, or even "meninists"—a global group of men who, according to Feminist.com, "believe in and support the feminist principles of women's political, social and economic equality." These are people who understand that men are not born on Mars and women are not born on Venus but, rather, that we are all born on the same planet as equals. Like male feminists, men who are allies actively support gender justice. They "believe that women as a group suffer inequalities and injustices in society, while men as a group receive various forms of power and institutional privilege," writes Australian scholar Michael Flood in his pro-feminist FAQ. These antisexist men resist using the term "feminist" in describing themselves because, while they support gender equity and oppose sexism, they see their role as supporting women who have done feminist work for so long. Pro-feminists want neither to colonize feminism nor to act as if they've got all the answers.

There's no reason to shy away from claiming the term "feminist," though our commitment to sociopolitical improvement may be more important than what we call ourselves. A person can be political without a label and sometimes we might not want to be tied down by a label at all. But particular labels can tell us about a person's politics. And when it comes to the long history of feminist efforts, there have been many men working alongside women in the struggle for gender equality.

Chapter 2

The Men's Auxiliary:
A Brief History of Men and Feminism

In 1776, the United States incorporated a limited version of egalitarian principles in the Declaration of Independence by including the phrase "all men are created equal." Abigail Adams implored her husband, John Adams, to "remember the ladies" and grant civil rights and representation to all women under the nation's new Constitution. As much as he loved Abigail, and as strongly as he believed in the principles of freedom, John replied to Abigail's letter by writing that the framers of the Constitution knew better than to repeal the "masculine systems." Loosening the bonds of male-run government, he wrote, "would completely subject us to the despotism of the petticoat."

"You must remember," Abigail wrote back, "that arbitrary power is like most other things which are very hard, very liable to be broken; and, notwithstanding all your wise laws and maxims, [women] have it in our power, not only to free ourselves, but to subdue our masters, and without violence, throw both your natural and legal authority at our feet."

By limiting their vision of equality to white men, the founders set women and people of color on a long road to achieving equal rights. It would take more than a century for the U.S. government to begin extending the benefits of legal equality to all. This goal still has yet to be fully accomplished, and women continue to face economic, political, social, and sexual inequities that are often compounded by virtue of race and class. For centuries, women have tirelessly confronted these issues, and men in the United States and around the globe have joined in their efforts.

This chapter highlights the history of men and feminism in the United States, although feminism—and men's role in it—certainly doesn't begin or end in America. There are powerful examples of men throughout history and from nations around the world who stood as allies in women's fight for autonomy and civil rights. Ancient Greece had Plato, Qasim Amin wrote from Egypt, John Stuart Mill famously supported British women's rights, and August Bebel and Friedrich Engels represented German socialists' support for equality. These men and others spoke out about marriage and education, suffrage, women's right to own property and businesses, and for women's opportunities to earn the same wages for the same work that men did. Some staunchly supported sexual liberation, birth control, the freedom to make decisions about one's own body, and women's fundamental right to free expression. More recently, antisexist men started also focusing on social equality, including sexual abuse, pornography, male violence against women, and the role of women in religion.

Michael Kimmel and Thomas Mosmiller's collection of primary documents, *Against the Tide: Pro-Feminist Men in the United States, 1776–1990, A Documentary History*, includes more than one hundred first-person quotes from pro-feminist men such as Thomas Paine, John Dewey, Ramon Sanchez, Upton Sinclair, Rabbi Stephen Samuel Wise, Omar Elvin Garwood, W. E. B. Dubois, Reverend Luther Lee, and members of the Pi Kappa Phi Fraternity.

Although many of these men benefited from the privilege of their sex, many simultaneously experienced oppression *from* other men— and sometimes from women—based on their race, religion, class, or sexual orientation. In the past—as it remains today—these men struggled with the condition of being both oppressed and oppressor. Kimmel and Mosmiller explain that even if men wield power over women because of their gender status, some men lack power in other regards and "have also had their own histories distorted, repressed, or obliterated." Many of these men were able to see the links between their own oppression and the gender-based oppression of women.

A Brief History of Feminism in the United States

Since Abigail and John Adams's correspondence about women's rights in the spring of 1776, the women's rights movement and its male allies have continued a long, rich, imperfect, and sometimes controversial history. To understand men's role in the feminist movement, it's important to first have an overview of the movement itself, which has been led and primarily populated by women.

U.S. feminism is generally divided by historians into three "waves," during which activism surged. The period during the late nineteenth and early twentieth centuries is known as the first wave of feminism and focused primarily on suffrage. Many of the early suffragists were active in the movement to abolish slavery in the United States and began to examine their own oppression as women. In addition to fighting for the vote, women's rights activists of the nineteenth century addressed inequities in education, employment, marriage, and many other areas of life.

The feminist second wave started in the 1960s and lasted through the mid-1970s. This era coincided with the free speech, civil rights, and anti–Vietnam War movements. Students took to the streets demanding rights for women and all underrepresented groups. Women's rights and liberation groups fought to end sex segregation in hiring, to achieve equal pay for equal work, to acknowledge and end domestic violence and rape, to share housework and child rearing equally with men, to legalize abortion, to extend rights to lesbians, and to end the sexual objectification of women. Books about women's history, personal politics, and self-defense were published at a rapid pace. Activists fought to reclaim control of women's health by educating women about their bodies, pushing for women's inclusion in health studies, establishing health clinics, and making birth control and reproductive information accessible. In 1970 the first women's studies program started, at San Diego State University.

Plato in Ancient Greece

In most city-states of ancient Greece, women had few political rights. They could not vote or own property, and most were under the control and protection of their husbands or fathers. Girls from Sparta were the only females who were provided an education through the state. The women of ancient Athens were cut off from the duties and rewards of citizenship and, except for courtesans and priestesses, were largely confined to the home. Women lived in special sections of the house that were remote and protected. Men's and women's quarters each had their own entrance.

Set in this context, the Greek philosopher Plato (428–347 BCE) is an early example of a man who challenged the status quo and, in some ways, championed women's rights. Plato was born into a distinguished family and probably never married. He had an excellent education and became a student of Socrates. Among his significant body of work, Plato's writings on women focused on women's roles in relation to political and moral principles of justice and virtue and the best way to create the greatest possible state.

In 360 BCE Plato wrote *The Republic*, a famous reflection on justice, the state, and the human soul. In *The Republic* Plato wrote that women are fully equipped to participate in all the functions of a citizen, including those of the guardian class or even the Philosopher King, the leader who relies on wisdom to rule the city-state. Men and women alike possess the same qualities, Plato wrote. "They differ only in their comparative strength or weakness," he claimed in Book V of *The Republic*. In a radical departure from the practices of his time, Plato advocated education for girls: "If the difference [between women and men] consists only in women bearing and men begetting children, this does not amount to a proof that a woman differs from a man in respect to the sort of education she should receive; and we shall therefore continue to maintain that our guardians and their wives ought to have the same pursuits."

In contrast with other ancient philosophers, such as Aristotle, who thought women were naturally inferior and lacked the capacity to reason, Plato argued that it benefits society when women are fully engaged in the life of the state. He also recognized, however, that this would never happen if women were continually loaded down by unequal responsibility for housework and domestic chores. To solve this problem, Plato developed theories about education, public housing, child rearing, and marriage—and the division of labor between men and women—that would create an ideal city in order to maximize citizens' happiness and create a just state. Plato proposed his idea in the form of a question, asking, *If women are to have the same duties as men, then shouldn't they also be provided the same training and education?* Plato suggested that children should be raised in state-run nurseries and women should be trained in gymnastics, the military, and government.

Plato's ideas about women can be considered feminist and provocative—even if they are imperfect. Plato seems to be saying that women can be guardians along with men, presuming they possess the right qualities. At the same time, however, his views on the state's role in private life lead to troubling conclusions about individual autonomy. Plato wrote, for instance, that women should be allowed by the state to bear children from the time they were twenty until they turned forty. "Anyone above or below the prescribed ages who [engages in reproduction] shall be said to have done an unholy and unrighteous thing." Guardians of the state were to live communally by sharing their wives and families in common, an idea that many find problematic.

Philosopher Lynda Lange argues that Plato was not a feminist because his primary objective was to make the guardians more efficient and to promote state unity, rather than to create equality between women and men or to end women's subordination. Yet it remains that Plato's views on women were remarkably unconventional at the time.

The third wave, which revved up in the 1990s, continues the political and cultural changes initiated by activists and scholars in earlier years. Among other issues, activists have taken up questions about imperialism, global politics, race, sexuality, and gender parity. Some scholars and activists date the beginning of third wave activism to the clinic defense movement and responses to the backlash against abortion rights; others date it to Anita Hill's sexual harassment testimony during the Senate hearings to confirm Clarence Thomas's appointment to the Supreme Court. Some say that the third wave formed partly in response to the perceived separatism of the second wave; others argue that third wavers object to the second wave's privileging of white women's concerns and have expanded on the work written by women of color feminists in the late 1970s and the 1980s.

Parsing history into waves helps us make sense of the long feminist legacy, but there are drawbacks to using this shorthand. This framing does not apply to feminist history around the world. It also creates tendencies to overlook the centuries before first wave feminism as well as the decades between the waves. During these eras, concern about women's political, social, and economic status existed—even if this interest did not garner as much public attention as the women's suffrage movement at the turn of the twentieth century, the street demonstrations for equality in the 1960s, or the clinic defense protests in the 1990s.

Just as the wave construct downplays activities in the "mid-wave" periods, it also mutes men's historic role in feminism. Many men who joined the women's rights movements were intellectuals and artists, commentators and astute social critics who got involved with women's rights issues through engagement with broader social activism. Social justice concerns never entirely disappear, and justice movements tend to be tied to other, similar political efforts. Yet that doesn't mean these endeavors come easily. As Kimmel and Mosmiller note by the title of their documentary history, strong sociopolitical forces are at work to preserve masculine power and advantage. Feminist men (and women) have worked *against the tide* of mainstream U.S. culture.

Práxedis Guerrero, "The Woman"

Born to a wealthy land-owning family in Los Altos de Ibarra, Guanajuato state, Práxedis Gilberto Guerrero (1882–1910) was a Mexican revolutionary who fought dictatorship and oppression. Guerrero was educated through secondary school and later worked as a laborer. He was a member of the Partido Liberal Mexicano (PLM) and died tragically at the age of twenty-eight while leading a group in the fight against President Porfirio Díaz at the dawn of the Mexican Revolution.

Shortly before his death, Guerrero wrote "The Woman," an essay about the highest ideals of human freedom and the role of custom as women's enemy.

Women cannot live as free companions of men because custom opposes it, because violation of custom brings disdain, mockery, insults and curses. . . . [B]ecause of this, the emancipation of women encounters a hundred opponents for every man who defends it or works for it.

Free equality does not try to make men out of women; it gives the same opportunities to both halves of the human species so that both can develop without obstacles, supporting each other naturally, without taking away rights, without usurping the place each has in nature. We men and women must fight for this rational equality, which harmonizes individual happiness with collective happiness, because without it there will always be a seed of tyranny in the home, the sprout of slavery and social misery. If a custom is a yoke, let us break with that custom no matter how sacred it may seem.

Guerrero's essay is revolutionary and radical, yet he was a man of contradictions. Guerrero rejected ideas that women were inferior to men. He confronted custom and prejudice as the source of perpetuating women's second-class status. However, "The Woman" also contains essentialist assumptions about men's and women's allegedly natural differences. Guerrero believed in conquering injustice, but he also rejected masculinity in women and femininity in men. He was a revolutionary, but he titled a critical article directed against former PLM member Antonio Villarreal "Que Hable el Maricón" ("May the Fag Speak").

Women's Suffrage

In 1848, abolitionists Lucretia Mott and Elizabeth Cady Stanton organized the Seneca Falls Convention in New York. Mott and Stanton had met eight years earlier at the World Anti-Slavery Convention, where they, along with all other women attending, were not seated as delegates because of their sex. The Seneca Falls Convention brought together approximately three hundred people, including forty men, to address women's rights. The event resulted in the Declaration of Sentiments and Resolutions, a document that articulated the goals of the early women's movement, including access to education and the professions, the right to own property and retain wages, egalitarian divorce laws, and the right to vote.

Along with Mott and Stanton, many of the men who supported women's right to vote were drawn to the movement through their engagement with antislavery activism. As Kimmel and Mosmiller point out, these men included white abolitionists such as Reverend Samuel May and Wendell Phillips as well as many black abolitionists, including Charles Redmond and Robert Purvis.

At Seneca Falls, abolition leader Frederick Douglass played a key role in persuading the attendees to include female suffrage in the Declaration of Sentiments. Partly because of conversations with Stanton, Douglass concluded that excluding women from the political

The Company of Men in the Procession.
(Photos by the Pictorial News Co.)

Despite opposition in the broader culture, some men worked actively to help secure women's right to vote. Here, a group of men marches in a suffrage parade in New York City in 1911.

process and denying them the right to vote were actions based on stereotypes, assumptions about "woman's sphere," and the so-called indelicacy of women's participation in politics.

At the time U.S. culture was largely set up to support the idea of separate spheres—that women were "naturally" best suited for housework and child rearing, baking, nurturing, and all other domestic activities. People who supported separate-spheres ideology believed women's place was in the home because they were naturally submissive, pious, and pure. Possessing these so-called feminine qualities was used as an excuse to keep women from participating fully in the public sphere. Some believed these traits made women unfit for taking part in the rough-and-tumble world of politics and the economy. By this logic, the public realm was reserved for men, who, it was thought, had the natural moxie to handle conflict and competition.

Douglass argued against these justifications for women's disenfranchisement. "I have never yet," he stated, "been able to find one consideration, one argument, or suggestion in favor of man's right to participate in civil government which did not equally apply to the right of woman." Although Douglass's position on women's rights was complicated by his belief that black men should receive the right to vote first, he clearly articulated the political and ideological links between equal rights, abolition, and the women's movement. He supported emancipation, education, women's rights, and freedom from discrimination. These beliefs were illustrated by the slogan of his newspaper, *North Star*: "Right is of no Sex—Truth is of no Color."

In his 1881 autobiography Douglass wrote that seeing "woman's agency, devotion, and efficiency" in arguing against slavery drew him to the women's rights movement. "I am glad to say that I have never been ashamed to be" called a "woman's-rights" man, Douglass claimed. "Recognizing not sex, nor physical strength, but moral intelligence and the ability to discern right from wrong, and the power to choose

Women's Rights in England: John Stuart Mill

In England, political thinker and social reformer John Stuart Mill (1806–1873) contributed important ideas to the development of nineteenth-century feminist thought. He was an early supporter of women's right to vote in England, and as a civil libertarian, Mill argued that women were deprived of their freedom and dignity by the state and by social custom.

In 1869, Mill published *The Subjection of Women*. (It is widely recognized that Mill's partner, Harriet Taylor, was instrumental in developing the ideas about liberty, justice, and the subjection of women that became the core of Mill's essay.) Mill contended that women's unequal political status could not be justified by claims about women's so-called feminine nature because what was known about women's "nature" was entirely shaped by the inequalities under which they had always lived. In other words, Mill was an early anti-essentialist feminist thinker.

Mill famously wrote that a society that keeps half its people in subjection could never hope to be a just society. To justify subjection by claiming that women are physically weaker than men amounts merely to barbarism. At the same time, justifying chivalry or male generosity with the fact that *some* women have less muscular strength than *some* men is merely the same barbaric argument in disguise. As feminist historian Rosemary Agonito explains, Mill believed that control by the male sex that is based on paternalism "uses bribery and intimidation instead of brutality to secure obedience, deference, and gratitude for protection. This bribery and intimidation is effected by rendering women economically and morally dependent on men. The law completes the intimidation by its discriminatory statutes," thus creating conditions in which the position of women is like that of slaves.

To Mill, the situation of married women was even worse than what slaves faced. "No slave is a slave to the same lengths, and in so full a sense of the word, as a wife is," Mill wrote. Describing marital rape, Mill explained that wives at the time had no recourse to "refuse to her master the last familiarity. . . . [H]e can claim from her and enforce the lowest degradation of a human being, that of being made the instrument of an animal function contrary to her inclinations." A wife, like black slaves in America, had no legal rights over herself or her own children.

In 1867, Mill proposed an amendment to the Reform Bill before British Parliament that would give women the vote. Mill's efforts were defeated by the all-male Parliament. Decades after Mill argued for women's suffrage, other men joined the cause. In *The Men's Share? Masculinities, Male Support and Women's Suffrage in Britain, 1890–1920*, Angela John and Claire Eustance identify more than one thousand men who were members of various suffrage groups. Most single-sex, or predominantly male, suffrage groups formed in England between 1907 and 1913. Left-wing writers Henry Brailsford, Laurence Housman, Henry Nevinson, and thirty-seven others formed the Men's League for Women's Suffrage in 1907; three years later they created the Men's Political Union for Women's Enfranchisement.

Men who got involved with these groups risked being called "unmanly" or cowardly. Yet men's support for the suffrage movement was extensive and diverse, even though it was complicated by limitations some men faced in critically challenging their own assumptions about masculinity. Some based their efforts on the idea that men's preexisting political power gave them a platform for being heard. Male suffragist Henry Nevinson unhappily stated to his friend Christabel Pankhurst that women would be able to win the vote only when men spoke up. Others in the movement were driven by less egalitarian motives, taking up the cause of the women's vote primarily out of chivalry and paternal protectionism—ironically, the same rationale used by men who opposed women's suffrage. Regardless of why men joined the cause of women's suffrage, the movement was considered radical on the part of all who were involved.

It wasn't until 1928, more than sixty years after Mill attempted to change the law to give women the right to vote, that British women were granted full suffrage rights.

between them, [are] the true basis of Republican government," Douglass continued.

Douglass believed that there was no reasonable excuse to exclude women, as he wrote, "from the right of choice in the selection of the persons who should frame the laws, and thus shape the destiny of all the people, irrespective of sex." Others, such as William Lloyd Garrison and Parker Pillsbury, sided with Douglass's politics, arguing that abolition and suffrage both promoted the inherent equality of all people.

The Men's League for Woman Suffrage, organized in 1910 largely by *The Masses* editor Max Eastman, created visible male support for women's right to vote and constituted the first pro-feminist men's group in the United States. The efforts of this group, along with the hard work of so many other men and women, were finally successful. More than seventy years after the Seneca Falls Convention, the Nineteenth Amendment, which guaranteed women the right to vote, was ratified in 1920.

Marriage Reform and Free Love

Stereotypes and assumptions about separate spheres and "women's nature" had ramifications beyond women's fight for the vote. For instance, in the late 1800s medical experts claimed that women should be barred from college because studying would damage women's delicate constitutions. Doctors claimed that studying would suck vital blood to the brain from women's reproductive organs, making them (but not men) sterile and sexually unattractive.

Stories that women were less evolutionarily developed or that studying would cause women's ovaries to atrophy were simply ideological belief systems wrapped up in fake science. However, the consequences of these myths were real. Women were prevented access to higher education and were considered the property of their husbands well into the twentieth century. Many women opposed this oppression. Fortunately, there were men who did, as well, by writing about women's rights and questioning claims about women's so-called feminine nature. Feminist men cut through these myths and fallacies. Claims about women's essential character, they explained, were actually ideological justifications for political repression.

When it came to marriage laws, for example, separate-spheres ideology meant that in most cases, husbands had legal control over their wives. Women often could not own property in their own names, hold jobs, or keep the wages they earned when they were permitted to work. There were no laws regarding marital rape because it was commonly presumed that providing sex for her husband was part of women's domestic obligation, whether consensual or not.

Of course, the idea that women belonged in the home applied mostly to white women of some financial means; black women, immigrant women, and poor women had always worked outside the home. What united all women, however, was that all were barred from participating fully in the public sphere of civic engagement.

The women and men who campaigned on behalf of specific issues such as suffrage and education rights understood that social change required broad transformations in public laws *and* shifts in the private sphere and social relations. To that end, advocates for women's rights fought for the transformation of marriage relations and for improvements in the private sphere.

Progressive men joined women in pointing out that barring women from civic engagement was a problem, but *also* that the domestic sphere needed improvement. These men promoted egalitarian relations and encouraged improved marriage and divorce contracts. On April 2, 1832, author, politician, and social reformer Robert Dale Owen created a new kind of egalitarian marriage contract. On the day of his wedding he stated about his bride, "This afternoon I enter into a matrimonial engagement with Mary Jane Robinson, a young person whose opinions on all important subjects, whose mode of thinking and feeling, coincide more intimately with my own than do those of any other individual with whom I am acquainted." Owen promised his new wife that he was renouncing the unjust, unearned marital privileges (such as sex at will or control over all the family money) that

Feminism and German Socialism

Feminist thinkers tended to draw their ideas and concerns from what they knew about their own lives and the world immediately around them. This often meant that women's rights spokespeople, particularly those who came from privileged socioeconomic backgrounds, didn't address the conditions of those outside their own social class. Feminist scholar Alice Rossi explains that members of the women's movement "wrote and spoke as if they were equally concerned with women at all levels of society," but their feminism was actually linked to their class status.

For German socialist feminists, however, economic and class analysis was central to their critique of women's political status. Socialist feminists drew important parallels between the condition of women and that of the working class and suggested radical solutions to wipe out the oppression of both.

German political thinker Friedrich Engels (1820–1895), for example, argued that economic arrangements—not women's so-called feminine nature—kept them subjugated. He and his close collaborator, Karl Marx, used the concept of historical materialism (a way of studying economics, history, and society) to explain the brutal abuse of the working class. Engels developed a systematic explanation for women's condition in his book *Origin of the Family, Private Property and the State* (1884).

Engels grounded his argument in the philosophical perspective that first, all social and intellectual relations are explained by the material condition (i.e., how goods and services are produced and distributed). Second, the most basic material condition is the economic structure. What Engels meant by this was that how we shop (for example, online or at a brick-and-mortar store, or through barter and exchange), what we buy (Dolce&Gabbana, organic yogurt, or fast food), and how we produce the "stuff" for sale (are we working in isolated cubicles or producing wheat on a family farm?) influences our social relations with each other and how we understand our world. In the case of women, the economic structure hinges on family relations and the ways in which these arrangements exploit women's labor. To Engels, the first class struggle was between men and women within the family, where the man is the bourgeois and the woman is the proletarian.

August Bebel (1840–1913), leader of the Social Democratic Party of Germany from 1869 to 1913, was another German socialist who melded economic and gender analysis. Self-educated and working class, Bebel unequivocally supported women's rights.

Bebel's main argument was that socialism was necessary in order to achieve equality between the sexes. His focus was on rights for working-class women, specifically. His book *Women and Socialism*, first published in 1879, articulates these views on women in society. Bebel argued that "bourgeois suffragists" were deluded if they thought getting the vote would solve their problems. Even with suffrage rights, Bebel explained, women would still be held down by the sex slavery of marriage and prostitution, and the vote wouldn't create economic independence for married women. Bebel emphasized that marriage should be understood as a private contract between two fully equal partners. These partners should be able to dissolve their own contract at will and without external constraints when the relationship between the two made it necessary.

While there are positive aspects of these socialist thinkers' ideas, there are also limitations. Engels has been criticized for his naturalizing perspective on women. And although he wrote grand theories about the oppression of women within the family system, Engels seemed unaware of his own sexism in relating to women in his personal life. Finally, there are limits to socialist perspectives because putting most of the blame for oppression on capitalism doesn't address all the ways that gender inequality manifests. Nor do Engels's and Bebel's versions of socialist feminism account for racism. In the end, while no perfectly socialist state has existed, gender inequality has not disappeared within socialist countries.

were conferred upon him by virtue of his being male. Instead, he was entering into a partnership of equals.

"I can not legally, but I can morally divest myself," Owen wrote. "And I hereby distinctly and emphatically declare that I consider myself, and earnestly desire to be considered by others, as utterly divested, now and during the rest of my life, of any such rights, the barbarous relics of a feudal, despotic system," he vowed. Owen's forward-thinking marriage contract was a powerful example of an antisexist man recognizing the importance of men's position in relation to power.

In a similar statement written by newlyweds and social reformers Lucy Stone and Henry Brown Blackwell, the couple honored their new marriage yet protested unjust marital laws and customs. In 1855, the couple wrote, "We believe that personal independence and equal human rights can never be forfeited, except for crime; that marriage should be an equal and permanent partnership, and so recognized by law; that until it is so recognized, married partners should provide against the radical injustice of present laws, by every means in their power."

After a cross-cultural look at women's status in British, French, and U.S. literature, Stone and Blackwell's contemporary, abolitionist Theodore Dwight Weld, concluded that limitations in women's mental and physical performance were the *result* of oppression, not the excuse for it. Unitarian minister Jesse Jones added in 1874 that while legal change was important, getting the right to vote, for example, was not primarily a political question but a social one. Really changing society, Jones explained, requires "a profounder revolution in the whole structure of society than many advocates seem ever to have dreamed of."

Years later a man by the name of Hutchins Hapgood published a short article in the *Chicago Evening Tribune* titled "Learning and Marriage" (c. 1915). Hapgood pointed out that women professors in the country's universities tended to stay single. The reason for this, he explained, was that social expectations demanded that women choose between work and motherhood. (Interestingly, Hapgood conflated marriage with motherhood.)

At the time, people commonly thought that a professional, wage-earning woman would make a bad mother. Poor and working-class women had always worked, and so this belief reinforced class-based stereotypes that poor women were irresponsible mothers. Not true, wrote Hapgood: "It is beginning to be seen that women who work independently are, as a rule, more capable mothers and more interesting and attractive wives than those women who do not." (Notable again that Hapgood melded the benefits of wage earning with improvements in motherhood.) Forcing women to choose between paid work and marriage is a horrible burden, and one day, Hapgood claimed, would be recognized "as one of the barbarities of our time."

While some activists sought to reform the institution of marriage, others rejected it entirely in favor of what they called "free love"—the idea that sex and relationships could take place outside the confines of marriage, especially since marriage involved state control over personal choices. Notable women and men of the eighteenth and nineteenth centuries who supported free love included writers and philosophers such as Mary Wollstonecraft, Josiah Warren, Moses Harman, his daughter, Lillian Harman, Benjamin Tucker, and others. Some of these writers and thinkers drew their beliefs from anarchist principles, others more directly from feminist understandings about how marriage laws restricted women's freedom and autonomy.

By the early years of the twentieth century in New York City's Greenwich Village a simmering sexual revolution was taking place. A bohemian avant-garde promoted sexual autonomy for women and men, which led to radical changes in mores and relations. Influenced by the works of Karl Marx, Sigmund Freud, and Friedrich Nietzsche, this loosely connected group of intellectuals foreshadowed contemporary ideas linking sexual and social freedom with political and economic liberation.

According to historian William O'Neill, free love ideas among socialists, anarchists, and other progressives had a particularly feminist hue. Among New York bohemians, free love strengthened the position of young women, O'Neill wrote, and feminism had a lot to do with it.

Feminism in the Arab World: Qasim Amin

In 1863, Qasim Amin was born to a Turkish Ottoman father and an Upper Egyptian mother. Amin received a top-notch education in Alexandria and Cairo before studying law in France. He eventually got involved in the nationalist reform movement opposing colonialism. Amin's concerns about political domination led him to consider important concepts such as rights, justice, and equality. By the turn of the twentieth century Amin was a judge—and a staunch critic of Western imperialism. Amin's arguments against imperialism and Western colonialism emphasized women's emancipation as a core component in any successful struggle against foreign colonialism and cultural repression. Amin wanted women to develop intellectually so they could better educate their children, particularly their sons. His ideas about women's emancipation and republican motherhood were primarily aimed at a privileged upper-class elite. Until his death in 1908, Amin's goal was to blend nationalist and feminist ideas into a cohesive argument for improving society and strengthening the country.

In 1899, Amin published his pioneering book *The Liberation of Women (Tahrir al-Mar'a)*. Amin believed that freeing Egyptian society from what he called "its inferior position" first required liberating women. He argued in this book that veiling practices should be reformed, that women should not be secluded, and that arranged marriage and repressive divorce laws should be modified in order to improve women's status. Amin criticized

Free love was intended to put women on equal terms with men, and a free relationship of equals would supposedly be more durable and satisfying than, as O'Neill put it, "either a quick, tawdry affair or a traditional marriage with all its grey, authoritarian overtones."

Yet early-twentieth-century articles from the radical underground magazine *The Masses* reveal that these issues were worked out as imperfectly in the past as they remain today. While bohemian men were free to philander, a sexual double standard meant that women in this circle paid a high price in terms of their reputations and relationship options. Feminist and radical Floyd Dell, for example, initially supported free unions and nonmarital sex. But as the years these practices as un-Islamic, claiming they were counter to the actual intentions of Islam and created conditions for women that mimicked slavery. The primary step toward women's liberation, Amin wrote, was to educate women so that the mind could become free from harmful traditions and superstitions. In this way, women could maximize their contributions to society and their families.

In response to the many criticisms he sustained for arguments in *The Liberation of Women*, Amin developed his ideas more completely in his next book, *The New Woman (Al-Mar'a al-jadida)*, published in 1900. Amin's writings on women's emancipation continue to influence women's political movements in Islamic and Arab communities around the world.

His writings also evoke enormous controversy. Amin is considered by many to be the "father of Egyptian feminism." However, some disagree with this characterization. Harvard scholar Leila Ahmed notes that at the time Amin wrote, upper-class Egyptian society was intensely gender segregated. His depiction of women as "backward" or ignorant would therefore have been based on limited interactions with women. In contrast to the aristocratic elite, working-class and rural women were only partially veiled or secluded, if at all. His writings reveal elements of class bias and an effort to improve Egypt's "image and social position and its relations with the British," authors Malek Abisaab and Rula Jurdi Absiaab comment. Nonetheless, despite the limitations of his perspective, it is significant that Amin's early feminist ideas continue to generate interest and debate.

wore on, Dell decided this kind of feminism was a mistake because he thought it was anti-male. "By encouraging feminism in hopes of forming women who would be better companions and playmates," O'Neill reports, "Dell felt men were really hastening the day when women would be able largely to do without them."

No doubt, there were men in the past who walked their feminist talk when it came to women's sexual liberation. Yet Pauline Bart, reviewing Ellen Kay Trimberger's essay on sexual liberation, reports that despite men's engagement with the protofeminist sexual revolution of the early twentieth century, so-called "progressive men who claimed to want egalitarian relationships with intellectual women with whom they could both talk and kiss, left them for traditional women." Bart writes, "Apparently equality isn't sexy—good in their heads but not in their beds." Dell, for one, surprised his editorial colleagues at *The Masses* when his informal love partnership dissolved and he subsequently chose to get married, proclaiming that marriage was the superior institution and insisting that he'd in fact always believed in it.

When it came right down to it, the sexual rhetoric of progressive men often left women just where they'd started—facing rejection if they were intellectually successful or judgment if they chose to hook up with sexual partners without marrying them first.

Birth Control and Reproductive Rights

Along with suffrage, marriage, and sexuality, feminist-minded men also focused their attention on birth control and reproductive rights, understanding that improving health options for women was a political issue: Better reproductive choices meant improved life conditions for women, men, children, and families. Despite the tangled arguments about sexual liberation and free love that were incompletely resolved, some men spoke up on behalf of women's rights to autonomy and self-control over their bodies.

In the early 1800s, Robert Dale Owen wrote a book called *Moral Physiology*, which argued on behalf of birth control. Owen's is considered the first book in the United States to advocate birth control, but by this he primarily meant *coitus interruptus*. Elizabeth Cady Stanton—herself the parent to seven children—advocated voluntary motherhood and birth control (although she opposed abortion).

A vocal birth control movement emerged in the United States in the 1920s, led by Margaret Sanger, who promoted the idea that women should be free to choose when and if they have children. Many men supported the feminist campaign for birth control: Max Eastman, physician Ben Reitman (who was Emma Goldman's lover), William Sanger (husband of Margaret), Floyd Dell, and writer Denlow Lewis were a few of the key men who argued on behalf of a woman's right to decide when she chose to become pregnant or to have children. Their reasons, notes Michael Kimmel in *The History of Men*, generally rested on the belief that being able to choose when to have children would result in "happier babies." Early advocates also believed that birth control would promote "equality of sexual desire between women and men" and increase everyone's sexual satisfaction, Kimmel writes.

While intended to improve women's lives, the birth control movement was complicated by problems of racism and sexual politics. Sanger's critics have argued that eugenics and racism motivated her birth control work at a time when immigration policies included racial quotas and were blatantly biased against nonwhite, non-Christian, non–Western European immigrants. The feminist reproductive-rights movement thus developed against a complicated backdrop of gender, race, religion, and power and has inherited unresolved issues not only about women's rights but also about internal racism and politics within the movement.

Before the Food and Drug Administration approved the Pill in 1960, the primary options women in the United States had available to prevent (or try to prevent) pregnancy included abstinence, breastfeeding for long periods of time, men's withdrawal, and other ineffective folk remedies such as having sex while standing up, using potato slices as a diaphragm, or sneezing after intercourse.

The birth control pill changed sexual relations and increased women's sexual autonomy. For some, widespread availability of the Pill helped the free love movement pick up where it had left off earlier in the century. The Pill also meant that women could more accurately control when (or if) they wanted to have children. This had tremendous impact on the freedom it allowed sexually active, heterosexual women in choosing their goals and life paths. For all women, but especially for women of limited economic means or for those who were single parents, the Pill meant that women could better provide for the children they already had by effectively preventing unplanned pregnancies.

Like other aspects of sexual politics, abortion has also been a lightning rod for controversy. Terminating pregnancy, a medical procedure performed for any number of reasons, is a practice that has

Photograph by Tim Graham. © Hulton-Deutsch Collection/CORBIS

A group of "pregnant men" demonstrates at Queen's Road market as part of a birth control campaign in England in 1972. One of the men holds a sign depicting a "pregnant man" with the caption "WOULD YOU BE MORE CAREFUL IF IT WAS YOU WHO GOT PREGNANT?"

existed throughout history. Periodically, though, abortion has become a hot-button issue during times of backlash against women or in periods of general conservatism. Author John DeFrain writes in the *Macmillan Encyclopedia of Death and Dying* that from the 1600s to the early 1900s, abortion was not a crime in the United States if it was performed before fetal movement, which starts at about twenty weeks into gestation.

"An antiabortion movement began in the early 1800s," DeFrain writes, "led by physicians who . . . opposed the performing of abortions by untrained people, which threatened physician control of medical services." The controversy over abortion gained attention only "when newspapers began advertising abortion preparations" in the mid-1800s. DeFrain explains that marketing these medicines became a moral issue—not necessarily because of questions over when life begins—but because it was feared that women could use abortion to hide extramarital affairs. "By the early 1900s," DeFrain writes, "virtually all states . . . had passed antiabortion laws."

Despite historic (and contemporary) efforts to deny women access to abortion, there have been men who have consistently supported women's abortion rights as part and parcel of broader reproductive options available to women and their male partners. In a 1966 statement to the San Francisco Conference on Abortion and Human Rights, Dr. William Jennings Bryan Henrie argued bravely in public about the necessity of making safe and legal abortion available. Henrie explained that it was imperative that women be able to receive this medical procedure if and when needed. Henrie promised to continue providing abortions—even though he'd already been convicted of illegally performing the procedure. Henrie gave this statement seven years before the Supreme Court decision in *Roe v. Wade* (1973) made abortion legal in all states.

Radical Movements of the 1960s and 1970s

During the late 1960s and into the 1970s, radical political efforts were gaining momentum: The civil rights, free speech, and antiwar movements, the American Indian Movement, Chicano Liberation, and the Black Power movements took on the establishment and questioned the status quo. These politically radical groups, however, were not exempt from sexism within their own ranks, and the women's liberation movement formed in part out of specific demands for women's rights but also as a way to confront the sexism women experienced as members of other radical or progressive political groups.

The New Left, for example, a primarily student-led movement that promoted social activism to counter conservative politics of the 1960s, contained its own brand of sexism and unexamined racism. Because of this racism, some black activists separated from New Left organizations to form separatist Black Power groups. Many women also branched out after New Left men were passively resistant and even overtly hostile toward women. In 1969 activist Marilyn Salzman Webb was invited to speak about the burgeoning women's movement at a rally against the Vietnam War. During this speech, fistfights broke out in the audience and Webb's male comrades from the New Left started yelling, "Fuck her! Take her off the stage! Rape her in a back alley." Male leaders did nothing to subdue the crowd, author Judith Newton explains in *From Panthers to Promise Keepers,* "and many New Left women saw this as the last straw."

Some men recognized their own chauvinism and joined the women's liberation movement as pro-feminist allies. These men often took action against sexism after learning about misogyny through feminist women in their lives—wives, daughters, friends, or neighbors who brought political ideas close to home. Consciousness-raising— coming together to talk about the political aspects of experiences of such things as housework, birth control, rape, or relationships— was a key element in the process of realizing that "the personal was political." Men who got involved with women's rights recognized that so-called "women's issues" were indeed men's responsibilities, too. Whether or not these men called themselves feminist, they began doing work of their own to examine privilege, sexism, and men's role in making change happen.

By the 1970s, the women's liberation movement was moving full steam ahead. In 1972, John Lennon made the point, however, that even with *some* political gains, men still didn't recognize women as their social equals. Men had a lot of work to do, Lennon said, when it came to investigating their own chauvinism. Using a phrase coined by Yoko Ono, Lennon controversially announced on Dick Cavett's eponymous television talk show that "woman is the nigger of the world."

In a song by the same title, Lennon and Ono sang on Cavett's stage, "If she won't be a slave, we say that she don't love us / . . . While telling her not to be so smart we put her down for being so dumb." Lennon and Ono used jolting language to shock listeners into paying attention to the similarities between sexism and racism. In doing so, however, Lennon elided race and gender. Framing the issue by claiming that *all* black people shared the conditions of *all* women ignored the distinctions between race and gender and effectively made black women disappear from the equation. The movement still had a long way to go.

Gay Men's Support for Women's Liberation

Sexual double standards for women existed well before the sexual revolution of the early twentieth century and lasted long after. Many—though certainly not all—gay men understood that gay liberation and women's rights were connected by social and political similarities. Both groups faced discrimination and stereotyping, and many chose to confront these problems through organizing.

A few gay men's groups were vocal in their support of women's liberation. One of these groups was the Radical Faeries, which formed in the late 1970s. Informed by Marxist, anarchist, feminist, and neopagan sensibilities, Radical Faeries began promoting cooperation and mutual aid among all people, claiming strong interest in what their "sisters" had to say about gender, sex, politics, and nature. "The feminist movement is a beautiful expansion of consciousness," author Joey Cain explained on behalf of the Nomenus Wolf Creek Radical Faerie Sanctuary. "As faeries," Cain wrote, "we enjoy participating in [feminism's] growth."

As the sexual double standards from earlier in the century continued to endure, radical gay activist Carl Wittman wrote in 1972 that women's liberation from such unattainable expectations was inextricably tied not only to sexual liberation but specifically to gay liberation. In an essay titled "A Gay Manifesto," Wittman wrote that "all men are infected with male chauvinism. . . . It means we assume that women play subordinate roles and are less human than ourselves." He argued, however, that male chauvinism was not as dominant a perspective among gay men. "We can junk it much more easily than straight men can," he wrote. "For we understand oppression. We have largely opted out of a system which oppresses women daily—our egos are not built on putting women down and having them build us up. Also, living in a mostly male world we have become used to playing different roles, doing our own shit-work. And finally, we have a common enemy: the big male chauvinists are also the big anti-gays."

In 1975, the National Organization for Men Against Sexism (NOMAS) formed when activists held the first National Conference on Men and Masculinity. As an offshoot of women's liberation groups, NOMAS was concerned in its early days about working for social equality, creating broader ways of thinking about masculinity and femininity, and finding ways of being men without having to dominate women and other men. The core principles of NOMAS establish this commitment. These tenets state: "We are not standing up as men to create a movement that cares only about men's sex role issues, or only about gay rights, or only about supporting women's fight against sexism. What is most special about our movement is that we have seen the connections between all these injustices, and are committed to ending all of them." Early members of NOMAS were at the helm of antisexist visibility. They created workshops about ending rape and sexual harassment, they supported the Equal Rights Amendment, and they took visible, organized stands on political issues of the day.

At around the same time that NOMAS formed, authors such as Jon Snodgrass, John Stoltenberg, Gene Marine, Michael Messner, and R. W. Connell published important books about men, masculinity, and sexism. With titles such as *A Male Guide to Women's Liberation* (1972), *A Book of Readings: For Men Against Sexism* (1977), and *Refusing to Be a Man* (1989), these activist-scholars made significant contributions to the contemporary men's feminist movement. These books critically examined assumptions about how men were expected to act and talk. They linked sexist masculinity to the problems of sexism itself, and they pointed out the ways in which the expectations of masculinity limited men's options in realizing their full human potential and creating positive relations with others. John Stoltenberg, for instance, famously wrote in his essay, "Why I Stopped Trying to Be a Real Man":

> *If everyone trying to be a "real man" thinks there's someone else out there who has more manhood, then either some guy has more manhood than anybody—and he's got so much manhood he never has to prove it and it's never ever in*

doubt—or else manhood doesn't exist. It's just a sham and a delusion.

As I watched guys trying to prove their fantasy of manhood—by doing dirt to women, making fun of queers, putting down people of other religions and races—I realized they were doing something really negative to me too, because their fear and hatred of everything "nonmanly" was killing off something in me that I valued.

Other men evoked parallels between sexism, racism, and freedom. In "The Struggle to Smash Sexism Is a Struggle to Develop Women," activist-author Kalamu ya Salaam linked the struggle for black liberation in the United States with women's liberation. Salaam wrote, "The struggle to eradicate sexism, develop women and establish progressive relationships between African-american women and men is, in our opinion, a key and critical aspect of our national liberation movement, a movement against capitalism, racism and sexism, and for African-american political self-determination and economic self reliance."

Mirroring the work already under way, particularly by women of color and feminist theorists of intersectionality (e.g., the Combahee River Collective, Gloria Anzaldúa, Audre Lorde), Salaam explained that liberation victories could not be achieved sequentially but were simultaneous and mutually reinforcing. "Either all of us must have access to political and economic power," he wrote, "or else we as a people are not free."

Separatism, Essentialism, and Male Antifeminism

At times, despite their best efforts, feminist men and progressive allies inadvertently reinforced sexism as much as they challenged it. Then, as now, well-intentioned men were sometimes blinded by their own underexamined socialization and positions of relative power. In other words, some men talked a good talk but didn't quite walk it.

As Kimmel and Mosmiller write, there were certainly men whose "*work* appears to support women but the *writer* of the work appears not to have supported feminism in his everyday actions." In other instances, they point out, "a particular writer, or even a specific work, supported feminist thinking on one issue and was opposed to that same perspective on another issue." Even more dramatic were those men who supported women publicly but mistreated them in their personal lives, as was the case of Ben Reitman, who vigorously supported his partner, anarchist Emma Goldman, in public, but who, behind closed doors, was tyrannical and "obsessive in his flagrant promiscuity."

Second wave feminism caused seismic shifts in gender relations in the United States, and men responded to these changes in myriad ways. Some men, such as those who formed NOMAS, created a men's movement to end sexism. Others reacted by forming men's groups dedicated to exploring masculinity and gender roles from men's perspective. Still others formed men's rights and fathers' rights groups that were overtly hostile to the goals of feminism.

In the late 1960s and the 1970s, lesbian and feminist separatists made a strong argument for women-only spaces. Separatism was an important strategy given the hostility and lack of understanding that some women experienced from some men. Men's separatist groups responded with exclusively (and not necessarily hostile) all-male bonding activities and separatist activities of their own. In general, these groups gave men an opportunity to explore their sense of constriction and the ways in which they were stuck in rigid gender roles.

This experience often led to some important insights. For instance, the issue of fatherhood and family life became the central focus of writers such as black nationalist Jawanza Kunjufu, whose work promoted mentoring young boys and embracing the idea that men ought to be loving, tender dads. Judith Newton writes that Maulana Karenga's Young Lions Program introduced male-only rites of passage that drew from African-inspired values emphasizing "unity, self-determination, collective work, responsibility, cooperative economics, creativity, and faith." These ideas would later become the cornerstone for the 1995 Million Man March in Washington, DC, which brought together male speakers from various political perspectives urging black men to be responsible husbands and fathers and to stop misusing women, children, and each other.

Most men's separatist groups, however, were primarily made up of white members who tended to ignore race and class privilege among men. And *all* separatist groups tended to reinforce essentialist, glorified myths about sexual difference. While men's groups wanted to reinvent masculinity, create new rites of passage, and promote what Newton calls "emotionally connected models of manhood," male bonding didn't always translate to "cross-gender alliance" or real political improvements for women.

In one example of this, a group of loosely connected men began to form what's called the mythopoetic men's movement. These groups concentrated on understanding men's situation through archetypal myths and poetry. They held men-only retreats and drum circles and single-sex sharing opportunities for men.

Men's separatist groups were made famous by Robert Bly through his 1990 book, *Iron John: A Book About Men*, and by Sam Keen's *Fire in the Belly: On Being a Man*, published in 1992. Bly and Keen both focused on liberating the male psyche from suffering and increasing men's connection with their so-called masculine essence. They claimed this could be done, in part, by severing from the need for approval from what they called the symbolic mother of spiritual mythology. Feminist women who objected to this viewpoint claimed this was an example of unexamined woman blaming. The presumption that a "spiritual mother" had that much control over men's well-being was critiqued for being a spiritual spin on the blatant sexism and mother blame that already existed in the broader culture.

This movement has sustained serious critique through the years. Mythopoetic men's groups evoke the problems (and the benefits) that emerge with any separatist movement. Andrew Willis writes that mythopoetic groups "are more about glorifying traditional masculinity than exploring gender and male privilege." Nonetheless, many men have experienced emotional relief and personal growth through participating in groups such as these.

Many scholars argue that the mythopoetic men's movement was formed, in part, because of cultural anxiety that men began experiencing as a result of feminist achievements and a changing global economy. Men's economic losses put into stark relief questions about what it meant to be a man as corporate downsizing, a decline in real wages, and shifting gender roles challenged white, straight, middle-class masculinity.

With the movement's self-help emphasis, mythopoetic groups tended to focus on men's emotional and psychological well-being by encouraging men to get in touch with feelings they'd been forced to repress in our culture. In doing so, the movement helped to raise awareness about how strictly enforced gender roles and expectations hurt men as well as women; yet at the same time, it reinforced essentialist notions about men and women. And mythopoetic groups tended not to apply gender insight to political action. They didn't take outspoken positions on issues such as gay, lesbian, and trans rights, or family law issues such as divorce, domestic violence, or child custody.

Men's rights and fathers' rights groups, on the other hand, were formed with overtly political objectives. These groups argue that men's rights are infringed upon by unfair divorce and child custody laws, unjust domestic violence laws, and biased prohibitions against sexual harassment and rape. They claim that men are falsely accused of being abusers and that fathers are discriminated against in child custody cases.

Fathers' rights groups argue that the legal system is biased toward mothers. Parental alienation theory—the claim that one parent (usually the mother) tries to convince the children to hate the other parent, thus alienating the child from the noncustodial parent—is commonly used by fathers' rights advocates as "proof" that men face a stacked deck. The term "fathers' rights," though, is a misnomer. As researcher Michael Flood points out, there's a lot wrong with the fathers' rights movement. For one thing, their arguments privilege fathers' *contact* with children over children's *safety* from violence. "In short," Flood writes, "family law increasingly is being guided by two mistaken beliefs: that contact with both parents is in children's best interests in every case, and that a violent father is better than no father at all."

Moreover, men's rights groups claim that women make false accusations about abusive men. But according to Flood, men's rights groups actually lie "about the extent of women's false allegations of abuse or domestic violence." Men's and fathers' rights groups ironically blame feminism—a movement that aims to increase freedom—for constricting the rights and freedom of men.

Transitions

In contrast with the essentialist assumptions of men's separatist groups, the emergence of the transgender and queer movements has complicated simple binary understandings of masculinity, femininity, and gender. The trans and genderqueer communities tackle myths of sexual difference and question the idea that people are either male or female, all masculine or entirely feminine. In doing so, these activists have helped to further break down the idea that feminism is "just a woman's issue." Trans issues have specifically had an impact on feminist theory by expanding our concepts of gender, thus changing the assumptions and landscape of feminist theory and activism.

Trans people have always existed. But in the 1990s, transgender activism began informing new scholarship in ways that shifted the premise of trans status as a medical or psychological disorder. In *The Transgender Studies Reader,* scholar Stephen Whittle writes, "the questioning that trans people presented to others' identities [became] a growing challenge to all who place their confidence in the binary roles of sexed lives: man/woman, male/female, masculine/feminine, straight/gay." As a result, a slew of trans studies emerged linking feminist and queer theory. This work broadened the foundations for understanding that feminism is a political movement transcending "woman" as an essentialist subject. In other words, being interested in or concerned about feminist ideas and goals does not require that we identify with a particular gender, sex, or sexual identity.

Most broadly, as feminists of all genders began intentionally and critically analyzing all forms of injustice, the movement arrived at the understanding that feminism is a social justice movement intended to bust down the walls of inequity, constraint, and mandatory gender conformity. Feminism is about justice understood through the lens of gender.

Chapter 3

Constructing Masculinity:
Putting the How and the Why in the XY

FOR MOST PEOPLE, TALKING ABOUT GENDER is like a fish talking about water. Gender is such a huge part of our daily routine that we just take it for granted. For most of us, questioning how we "get gendered" occurs to us just about as often as we wonder whether the sun will come up. In other words, even though we're constantly creating and identifying gender roles, we don't tend to think about it.

Gender refers to the complex web of social meanings—qualities such as pretty, tough, or reckless—that are attached to biological sex. This process gets started early in our lifetimes—sometimes before we're even born, when parents decide how to decorate the nursery (pastel pink, blue, or yellow?) or when they choose a theme for baby shower invitations (baseball or fluffy bunnies?).

Feminism explains that masculinity and femininity are things we learn to perform, not behaviors we're born with. Gender shapes our relationships, skills, interests, and how we understand ourselves. But gender roles aren't carved in stone: We make them up. And because gender roles are culturally constructed, they can also be changed.

For example, we think of the color pink as gentle and soft—traits we associate with girls—and we think of the color blue as solid, firm, and tough—adjectives we link with boys. But the current pink-is-for-girls and blue-is-for-boys assumption wasn't uniform until the 1950s. In the past, these traits and colors were reversed. According to Jo Paoletti, an expert in textiles and American studies, people used to think that pink was masculine because it was a muted version of red, representing strength, the planet Mars, war, fire, and blood. Blue, on the other hand, was considered feminine because the color evoked peace, harmony, water, the sky, and Heaven.

Pink and blue—like so many other gender signifiers—are social conventions. We like our babies dressed in pink or blue. People tend to get anxious if the sex of a baby is not immediately obvious, argues Paoletti. But still, we'll take a baby in a gender-neutral pastel before we're likely to feel comfortable dressing a little boy in pink frills. This says a lot about how deeply invested we are in gender distinctions and about our attachment to the meanings and traits we associate with masculinity.

We carry in our minds plenty of unexamined presuppositions about masculinity and about what it means to be a guy. Ask people what they associate with masculinity and there's a good chance you'll hear responses such as guys are providers and protectors, they're physically strong, they're unemotional or emotionally reserved, and they're sexually in charge. They fix things, solve problems, kill spiders, and open jars. Violence and anger might even get thrown into the mix.

Yet along with deeply reinforced assumptions about gender, our culture also presents us with ambivalent—or contradictory—messages about masculinity. When it comes to being a guy, these are interesting times. Warrior masculinity is reinforced through military conflicts in Iraq, Afghanistan, and around the globe, while the term "metrosexual" also rolls easily off our tongues. So on the one hand, we have visions of rugged soldiers toughing it out in the elements and risking their lives to "protect and serve." At the same time, style magazines and movie stars promote images of men concerned with manicures, facials, and sleek, trim figures to carry off the latest fashion trends with aplomb. More American men are contentedly doing domestic work, but the popularity and aggressive excitement of men's mixed martial arts (MMA) is simultaneously at record highs. After four-on-the-floor MMA training, guys can tune in to TLC to watch Curtis

Stone, the Take Home Chef, whip up a crème brûlée with fresh berry topping (young men between the ages of eighteen and thirty-five are the coveted demographic for prime-time cooking shows). While this range of examples might represent an opening up of possibilities for how men want to live their lives, it also tells us something about our culture's anxieties around masculinity. So what does it mean to be a man in the twenty-first century, and what has it meant in the past?

High Heels or Combat Boots?

Gender expectations and ideals have shifted throughout history, and with them our ideas of what is "normal." For example, getting ripped and buff might be the style of the day, but these physical standards have changed through time. Hot studs in seventeenth-century France wore high-heeled shoes, red velvet jackets, and frilly white lace shirts, lots of blush, and white powder makeup. Particular ideas about masculinity existed in the 1600s, just as they do today. But instead of wearing high heels, a "guy's guy" today is more likely to wear sagging baggy pants or the latest in J. Crew gear. Depending on the scene, gay men might express masculinity through cars or gym memberships. Frat guys in Southern California often go for raised trucks, flip-flops, Axe body spray, and wraparound sunglasses to express their masculinity. It's no doubt pretty easy to picture badass punk guys with shaved heads and tough tattoos, or Latino lowriders with pimped-out cars, or attorneys with hard-shell briefcases and power to spare. In Jewish culture, men are often expected to accomplish the ideals of masculinity through savvy scholarly debate and professional or intellectual achievement. But all of these examples of masculinity are stereotypes, often replete with prejudices about class, race, and ethnicity. Media and niche advertising perpetuate these stereotypes even though most people don't conform to them. The reason? Because they represent an image, not real life.

Since gender ideals shift culturally and historically, through time and place, these stereotypes are called into question. Here's an example of one such stereotype exposed: In the early twentieth century, Jews were often denied entry to universities. Recent Jewish immigrants from

Eastern Europe were often poor or working class. Barred from higher education and facing poverty, they found that one available avenue for money and success was boxing, not a sport that's conventionally associated with Jewish men today. In fact, Jewish men aren't often associated with sports at all in the United States. In his book *When Boxing Was a Jewish Sport*, author Allen Bodner writes that between 1910 and 1940, there were twenty-six Jewish boxing champions, including men such as Benny Leonard, Barney Ross, and "Slapsie" Maxie Rosenbloom. By 1928 Jews were the majority ethnic group in U.S. professional boxing.

This example indicates not only that masculinity is historically contingent, but also that gender expectations and stereotypes are linked to ethnicity and class. References to the generic term "masculinity" often involve the invalid or unspoken assumption that when we say "men" we're talking about white, heterosexual, American, able-bodied, and middle-class people. This unexamined default setting reinforces privilege by making entire groups of men invisible.

We often also assume that masculinity equals dominance and aggression, a situation that social psychologist Robert Brannon sums up in three short words: no sissy stuff. This phrase dominates our collective imagination by invoking unrealistic expectations that men are by nature stoic, unemotional, aggressive, and interpersonally detached. Consistent with these stereotypes of masculinity, physical contact among men is never okay unless it takes place on the wrestling mat, on the football field, or in a fight. Author Clint Catalyst adds that "for males who don't pull off the role of 'straight-acting,' life isn't exactly carefree." In Catalyst's experience, the consequences of being a "sissy" have included sexual rejection, social ostracism, and even blatant job discrimination.

Hypermasculine ideology pressures guys to be bigger, stronger, faster, and harder. Summer of 2008 marked the release of *Bigger, Stronger, Faster*, a film about how American culture rewards speed, strength, winning, and being hard. In the United States, men are encouraged to do anything it takes to achieve these goals, to the extent that top athletes, high school students, and everyday gym rats are on the hot seat for taking performance-enhancing drugs. The media rightly point out that these drugs can be risky to people's health, but what often gets left out or glossed over in public debates about competition, performance, and steroids is how cultural assumptions about masculinity play into our ideas about being top dog and what it means to win.

Performance-enhancing drugs are a health issue, but they are also a gender issue. While some women are also incredibly competitive, taking steroids or amping up their athletic records by other dubious means, being bigger, stronger, faster, and harder is usually a guy thing. It is part and parcel of hypermasculine culture. And the pressure on guys to accomplish these traits shines a bright light on the social norms and ideas about masculinity that we often take for granted.

This picture of masculinity is restrictive to men and oppressive to all. Moreover, these default settings are just plain inaccurate. Conventional masculinity is a style of manhood that many men (and women) are complicit in upholding, although few actually embody. There is nothing traditional, universal, or eternal about our current conventions of masculine gender.

There are actually many versions of masculinity—not just the dominant mainstream model of hyperaggressive manhood. And what it means to be masculine can look very different depending on a person's sexual orientation, class, religion, ethnicity, or race. Masculinity comes in many forms and packages, which are also influenced by personal predilections. Clint Catalyst, for example, is a self-described prancy boy who favors flamboyant clothes and expressive affect. Stay-at-home dads may care for small children with tenderness. Writers, artists, and musicians can be thoughtful and perceptive. A dancer may be lithe, competitive, and hirsute; a bodybuilder might be burly, submissive, and hairless. The possibilities for how men select from the "gender buffet" are endless. Australian social scientist Raewyn Connell (herself formerly male) argues that there is not *one* true version of masculine identity. Instead, there are many aspects of, and multiple ways of performing, *masculinities*.

On Masculinity

Anyone with a handlebar mustache is a real man. Like Lemmy from Motörhead. That's a real man.

—Tyler Lewis, twenty-two-year-old student

To my Asian family, I am the eldest son and expected to act accordingly. My responsibilities namely include caring for my mother in her old age and watching my younger brother so long as he lives. On my white side, I am considered a flamboyant failure of a man, because I am not masculine enough. My white family expects that I'll marry a woman and have many children. Being queer puts quite a damper on this hope. I consider my manhood self-taught through life obstacles. Masculinity, in general, is nothing more than a guise. A mask that people hide behind to create a faux alpha-male positionality in society. It creates fear and intimidation. My natural butch/masculine appearance keeps people at a distance and works against me when talking to many gay circles who assume my sexuality is bent.

For me, the qualities of being a man include: an unyielding desire to grow as a human, a nurturing connection to all peoples, a constant struggle to understand my place as not being above any other person, and finally, being a man means constantly challenging any and all unconscious thoughts that are rooted in societal/cultural designs of misogyny. Being a man takes a lot of work because there is nothing natural about it. Manhood/masculinity/man are all performances. And performances take an awful lot of practice. Often those performances fail, other times they lead to an Oscar. Either way, masculinity is a performance of a lifetime.

—Benny LeMaster, twenty-seven-year-old barista

When I was about five years old, my father pulled me into the bathroom after dinner and told me to take off my clothes. I thought something was up because it wasn't my bath time and he had closed the door quickly,

as if he were trying to hide something. Being a kid, though, I took off my clothes and my dad took out a can of lime Barbasol and covered me from head to foot. I didn't like this at all and I tried to run out the door, but my dad grabbed me and told me that men should be hairy and that shaving me now would result in increased hairiness as I grew older. I didn't buy this for one second and started screaming for my mom. My dad tried to shut me up, but I kept crying louder until my mom yelled at my dad to open the door. She gave a little scream when she saw me standing there, covered completely in shaving cream and my dad with a razor in his hand, looking appropriately guilty. That crazy bastard.
—Ted Kim, thirty-nine-year-old news producer

According to Webster's American Dictionary College Edition, masculinity is defined as "pertaining to or characteristic of a man or men, such as strength or boldness." Last time I checked women could also have these qualities. I think we need more conversations about what masculinity means to both men and women.
—Cassie Comley, twenty-one-year-old student and surfer

My twenty-five-year-old male friend says masculinity is being strong physically and mentally. Being tough. But I'm not sure there is an easy way to define masculinity anymore. The thing is, just like women, men have always been changing what it means to define them. Physically, emotionally, psychologically, all men are different and we're always redefining ourselves. What makes one man feel more masculine might make another feel less so.
—Alaina Chamberlain, twenty-three-year-old community organizer

To me, masculinity is about everything I've done for the sake of feeling more comfortable with other men, feeling more attractive to women, or feeling that my father approves of me.
—Chad Keoni Sniffen, thirty-four-year-old sexual-assault prevention coordinator

It's even the case that masculinity is not something that only guys do. Women can be masculine, too. So despite all the stereotypes we might carry around in our heads, masculinity can actually take on many forms. And if that's the case, then what is masculinity and where does it come from? Can we change it? And would we want to?

The Nature/Nurture Debate

Biological factors contribute somehow to creating manhood. The question, though, is how much of being a man (or a woman) comes from nature and how much from nurture? The jury is still out on this question, but it's an important one.

Through the course of the twentieth century and into the twenty-first, arguments for nature or nurture as the primary explanation for gender have swung back and forth like a pendulum. In one era, social explanations take the lead in explaining human attributes. In the next generation, biology takes the front seat. We're now in the "nature" phase of this pendulum swing, so it's common to see headlines splashed across magazines and Internet sites emphasizing the so-called science behind masculinity and femininity and how men's and women's behavior is allegedly "hardwired." A 2007 FoxNews.com story exclaimed that men are "hardwired" to ignore their wives. In 2008 Star.com reported that men are "hardwired" to be extreme (whatever that means). Researchers at UCLA have claimed that women under stress are hardwired to form friendships with other women because of cascading brain chemicals. Some popular magazine articles even suggest that men are hardwired to cheat on their partners, which presumes that women never do and which provides a biological excuse for infidelity—a decidedly socially driven activity.

Historian Carl Degler writes in his book *In Search of Human Nature* that biological paradigms for explaining human behavior go in and out of favor depending on the ideological or political inclinations of an era. The focal points of biological explanations shift, too, so where biological arguments once focused on reproductive systems, the emphasis these days is on how the brain functions. This indicates that culturally these explanations serve to prop up what are largely ideological concepts of masculinity and femininity.

Biological models for understanding human behavior rely on the idea that innate biological differences between males and females "program" distinct social behaviors for men and women. This is called biological determinism. Socially based frameworks, such as those coming from the fields of cultural anthropology or sociology, look at variations in behaviors and gender attributes. These approaches highlight the socialization process that teaches boys and girls to live up to the expectations for their respective genders. Either approach on its own—biology or socialization, nature or nurture—is inadequate for explaining complex human beings and why we do what we do.

Science definitely has its place in helping us understand our biological selves. But in our culture these days science puts the seal of approval on issues that often have political components as well as biological ones. Ask evolutionary psychology expert Martha McCaughey or biologist Anne Fausto-Sterling about this, and they'll explain that science does not equal fact. Science equals fact plus ideology plus politics. As science writer Keely Savoie puts it in her blog, "Science—you slap that label on something and in most circles it instantly attains a level of credibility that almost nothing else can equal. But what trickles into the popular media as science news is far from infallible, following a circuitous process riddled with bias, judgment, and ideology."

Take, for example, the story of the sperm and the egg. This presumably innocent explanation of human conception is actually a profoundly gendered metaphor. The conventional sperm-and-egg rhetoric exposes how political ideas or cultural narratives can be foisted onto science.

The actual mechanics of conception are pretty straightforward: Egg meets sperm and meiosis follows. The story gets politically interesting, however, when we begin to think of sperm as male and eggs as female, imbuing sperm and eggs with gendered qualities. In our culture's narrative of conception, the ovum is described as "large and passive" and sperm are characterized as "active," "streamlined," and "strong."

Further scientific investigations, writes Annamarie Sheets of MIT, "have made it clear that these descriptions are influenced by cultural dualisms rather than observable data." Sperm come from men and eggs come from women, but that doesn't mean that sperm are masculine and that eggs are feminine.

Anthropologist Emily Martin explains that skewed imagery and gendered metaphors have permeated the story of reproduction. This illustrates "how cultural myths can turn into scientific myths, and vice versa." According to author David H. Freedman, who profiled Martin's work in *Discover* magazine, until very recently most biologists and school textbooks portrayed sperm as "intrepid warriors battling their way to an aging, passive egg that can do little but await the sturdy victor's final, bold plunge." In fact, when it comes to fertilization, Martin insists, "the egg is no passive lady-in-waiting." What's closer to the truth, Freedman reports, is this:

> *A wastefully huge swarm of sperm weakly flops along, its members bumping into walls and flailing aimlessly through thick strands of mucus. Eventually, through sheer odds of pinball-like bouncing more than anything else, a few sperm end up close to an egg. As they mill around, the egg selects one and reels it in, pinning it down in spite of its efforts to escape. It's no contest, really. The gigantic, hardy egg yanks this tiny sperm inside, distills out the chromosomes, and sets out to become an embryo. . . .*
>
> *Martin was surprised to find that popular literature, textbooks, and even medical journals were crammed with descriptions of warrior sperm and damsel-in-distress eggs. . . . Less mysterious, in Martin's opinion, was the motivation for such biased language. Men link potency to strong sperm, she says. You'd like your sperm to be like you; no wonder everyone believed sperm were torpedoes . . . [but] from the early 1970s on, studies of the sperm and eggs of many species have revealed that molecules released by the egg*

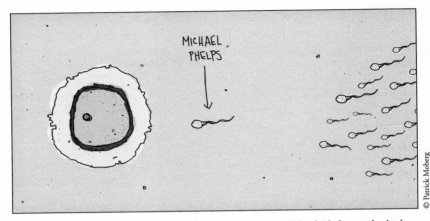

This cartoon, which jokes about olympic swim chapmion Michael Phelps, and which quickly spread on the Internet in 2008, humorously reflects cultural stereotypes that associate sperm with "masculine" traits such as competition and speed.

> *are critical to guiding and activating the sperm. . . . The notion of fiercely battling, competitive sperm suggests that they're battling each other in a race to the egg. . . . The macho image of sperm not only obscures this reality; it actually reverses what's been observed.*

What's significant is how masculine and feminine stereotypes are superimposed onto the sperm and egg. The resulting story of conception illustrates how we create and reinforce ideas about masculinity as aggressive and competitive. We shape science with our cultural ideas; in this case, science is not fact but fairytale.

Other times science is used to explain supposedly inherent traits of masculinity; these skewed biological explanations for what is perceived as gendered behavior must not be confused with fact. As McCaughey points out, these myths of masculinity wend their way into pop culture and politics specifically when arguments rely on so-called scientific experts to explain questions such as why men rape, why men dig big-breasted women, or why men like porn. When sociobiological theories are presented as science, McCaughey says, it reveals more about American culture than it does about scientific data. For instance, she reports that "Our Cheating Hearts," a 1994 *Time* magazine cover story on infidelity, offered an evolutionary explanation for why men cheat on their partners; *Muscle and Fitness* magazine used a theory of male and female sexual psychology in its 1994 article "Man the Visual Animal" to "prove" that men are born to leer at women; "The Biology of Attraction," featured in *Men's Health* magazine, explained to readers in 2005 that alleged primal evolutionary fertility signals give the green light to men to ogle young girls. Each of these justifications for *some* men's behavior provides, as McCaughey puts it, "a means by which heterosexual male readers can experience their sexuality as cultural [and] primal" through messages that tell men staring at women is biological destiny. These science-based rationalizations ignore other explanations for human behavior, such as how institutions and social practices create a context that gives men access to women's sexualized bodies.

Michael Kimmel writes in *Guyland: The Perilous World Where Boys Become Men* that boys and men face a complex social scene in which their attitudes, their relationships, their rules, and their rituals are shaped. This complex social scene includes everyday activities such as video games and music and even extreme events such as violent fraternity initiations, sexual predation, and school shootings. Masculinity is shaped through social institutions such as the military, marriage, pornography, mainstream sexuality, sports, work, pop culture media—and even science itself. But science-based explanations for behavior ask us to ignore these cultural and social influences.

In their introduction to *Men's Lives*, Kimmel and coeditor Michael Messner point out that the transformation from factual information to ideological story is a sleight of hand where "observed normative differences between women and men that are assumed to be of biological origin are easily translated into political prescriptions." In other words, "what is *normative* (i.e., what is prescribed) is translated into what is *normal*." This point is important. It is a magic trick that happens every day. And it has real consequences when science is used to justify what are actually cultural beliefs about gender.

When observed normative differences between women and men are assumed to have biological origins, we end up with arguments that reinforce stereotypes about gender and ultimately serve as excuses to keep women from achieving equality. For instance, author George Gilder argues that male sexuality is, by nature, "wild and lusty"—unless women control it. If women don't control men's sexuality, Gilder writes, they are abandoning their "natural" function. According to this line of thought, employment opportunities, sex education, abortion, and birth control all encourage women to turn their backs on their so-called natural roles.

Like Gilder, University of Virginia professor Steven Rhoads argues that gender equity is a pipe dream because men and women are born with different "natures." Rhoads relies on evolutionary theories to presume that any biological difference necessarily results in prescribed gender roles in the workplace, home, and family. Along similar lines, a June 2008 *Washington Post* article on education reported that boys and girls should be taught differently in school. According to family therapist Michael Gurian, brain studies show that boys don't hear as well as girls and that girls are more sensitive to light; boys fidget more and girls are more likely to behave and pay attention in class. Gurian and others such as Leonard Sax use these ideologically driven claims about how boys and girls are "hardwired" to promote sex-segregated classroom policy. But renowned education and gender scholar David Sadker counters Gurian's findings by calling them "stereotypes of the first order" that limit children's options and creativity.

Scientists and scholars such as Gilder, Rhoads, and Gurian are engaged in knowledge production. When biased perspectives on masculinity get picked up as quotes in pop culture outlets such as *Men's Health* magazine or the six o'clock news, scientific explorations become conflated with fact and we begin to assume that the suggestions of the "experts" are truth. Underlying bias or ideological assumptions get overlooked and, instead, biological arguments for men's behavior are commonly accepted as causal explanations. But the leap from discussions about biological differences to arguments that women and

The Caveman Mystique

Quips and quotes on gender issues provided to popular media by scientific experts become "part of popular consciousness, a sort of cultural consensus about who men are," writes Martha McCaughey in *The Caveman Mystique: Pop-Darwinism and the Debates over Sex, Violence, and Science*. These scientific explanations of gender become the cultural myths of our era. And, McCaughey points out, as French theorist Roland Barthes wrote in his book *Mythologies*, "Influential cultural myths work as taken-for-granted systems of meaning—particularly when people don't understand the historical conditions that gave rise to those myths." Without a historical context for understanding how scientific stories emerge to explain men's sexual behaviors and feelings, biology as destiny has become the paradigm through which many people understand men. McCaughey calls this the "caveman mystique."

The basic version of the mystique is that when humans lived in caves, men did the hunting and women gathered berries. This story becomes transformed into assumptions about human nature: If a man wanted sex, he threw a woman over his shoulder and dragged her back to the cave. We are told this is a biological imperative. This myth is used to justify all kinds of masculine sexual aggression, and it reinforces stereotypes about female passivity.

Myths of masculinity also use biology to prop up ideologies of gender

men *should* participate in different behaviors is misleading. There is no logical reason to assume that biology causes behavior in a linear fashion.

Does It Have to Be Either/Or?

Our ideas about masculinity and femininity run deep and are reinforced, in part, because of something called dichotomous thinking, or dualistic epistemology. What this means is that we tend to think in terms of opposites. We tend to structure our thought in pairs.

Binary categories often get overlaid with value judgments in which one side of the equation seems more important than the other. In our culture, masculine traits tend to be judged more worthwhile. This

difference. For instance, it's a biological fact that men can produce between fifty million and five hundred million sperm with each ejaculation
and women produce about four hundred mature eggs during the course
of their lives. The myth is formed when this factual information is used to
argue that men are thus biologically less "invested" in their offspring than
women are or that because of the biological differences in the number of
eggs and sperm produced, reproductive "success" for men means getting
as many women as possible pregnant in order to make good use of that
sperm. These kinds of narratives remove free will and morality from the
realm of human behavior.

As economic conditions deteriorate in the United States, the mythical
caveman identity—productive, protective, aggressive, and heterosexual—is
available to those whom McCaughey calls "men in crisis." As men confront
unemployment, corporate downsizing, and unstable economic markets, some
worry they are becoming less socially powerful. McCaughey writes that the
caveman mystique offers men a reassuring identity as virile, manly men.

Unfortunately, such Darwinian discourse is sometimes used to excuse
antisocial behavior. For example, one man, who was videotaped participating in New York City's Central Park group sexual assaults in the summer of 2000, is heard on video telling his sobbing victim, "Welcome back
to the caveman times." McCaughey wonders, How does a man come to
think of himself as a caveman when he attacks a woman? "What has made
so many American men [and women] decide that it's the DNA, rather than
the devil, that makes them do it?" she asks.

thought process generally does not occur on a conscious level, and
our presuppositions go unexamined. We don't think to ask important
questions, such as why we would choose *either/or* in the first place.
What if we revised how we structure knowledge to incorporate what
postmodern philosophers call the "both/and"? In other words, a revised
thought process wouldn't require dividing things into *either* nature *or*
nurture, yin *or* yang, good *or* bad, masculine *or* feminine. Instead, we
might conceptualize our surroundings as influenced by *both* nature
and nurture, yin *and* yang, good *and* bad, masculine *and* feminine.
Historically and around the world there are plenty of examples of
cultures that think of individuals as a blend of both masculine and

feminine traits, or that accept the existence of more than two genders. Anthropologist Margaret Mead explained as early as 1935 in her book *Sex and Temperament* that there are examples of cultures in which no one gender role was assigned to men or to women. Instead, each of us shares personality traits and temperaments and an infinite variety of human potential. In her essay, "Night to His Day," Judith Lorber expands on this issue:

> *Western societies have only two genders, "man" and "woman."*
> *Some societies have three genders—men, women, and*
> *berdaches or hijras or xaniths. Berdaches, hijras, and xaniths*
> *are biological males who behave, dress, work, and are treated*
> *in most respects as social women; they are therefore not men,*
> *nor are they female women; they are, in our language, "male*
> *women." There are African and American Indian societies that*
> *have a gender status called manly hearted women—biological*
> *females who work, marry, and parent as men; their social*
> *status is "female men."* . . . *They do not have to behave or dress*
> *as men to have the social prerogatives of husbands and fathers;*
> *what makes them men is enough wealth to buy a wife.*

Contemporary transgender debates add important perspectives to our conversations about masculinity and complicate our ideas about masculinity and femininity as either/or conditions. Transgender scholar Susan Stryker points out that while many people believe that masculinity is rooted in biology, the biological "cause" of gender identity has never been proven. Think of it this way, Stryker suggests: Humans have a biological capacity to use language, but that doesn't mean we're born knowing how to speak French. "Likewise," Stryker says, "while we have a biological capacity to identify with and to learn to 'speak' from a particular location in a cultural gender system, we don't come into the world with a predetermined gender identity."

Similarly, Judith "Jack" Halberstam proposes that masculinity cannot be reduced to the male body. The presence of what she calls "female masculinity" requires that we expand our limited gender categories to account for tomboys, butch lesbians, and other gender benders.

In her book *Dude, You're a Fag: Masculinity and Sexuality in High School,* author C. J. Pascoe explains that practices called "gender maneuvering" challenge our assumptions about masculinity. During a year and a half she spent hanging out in a working-class high school doing research, Pascoe noticed girls who appropriated clothing styles, sexual practices, and interactional dominance usually associated with boys, calling into question our assumptions that masculinity is the sole domain of men. These continuing debates confront essentialist assumptions about gender.

According to psychologist Sandra Bem's classic research on psychological androgyny, masculinity and femininity are in many respects orthogonal—not oppositional—to each other. In other words, instead of thinking about masculine and feminine gender traits and characteristics (which are also associated with sexual traits and characteristics, or assumptions) as being polar opposites on the same axis, we should actually visualize them as existing on different, perpendicular dimensions. Therefore, they are independently variable.

Bem rated people on two scales: One scale measured stereotypically female-ascribed traits and the other measured stereotypically male-ascribed traits. In asking respondents how strongly they rate themselves in possessing supposedly gendered traits—such as self-reliance, helpfulness, cheerfulness, loyalty, need for power, independence, or shyness—Bem found that many people score high on both scales. She also found that many people score low on both. And—most important—Bem found that a high score on one does not predict a low score on the other. What this means is that male does not equal masculine and female does not equal feminine. Instead, explains gender theorist Eve Kosofsky Sedgwick, some people are more *gender-y* than others. But there's no rigid, hard-and-fast thing called masculinity or femininity. Gender is constructed and it is changeable and it's something we can all

The Sexual Continuum: Why Male and Female Are Not Enough

Anne Fausto-Sterling, professor of biology and gender studies at Brown University, has written extensively on sexual and gender identity. In this excerpt from *Sexing the Body: Gender Politics and the Construction of Sexuality*, Fausto-Sterling writes about Levi Suydam, a young person who today might be described as intersex. This story provides an example of how two sexes—male and female—don't adequately describe the full range of human sexual existence.

In 1843 Levi Suydam, a twenty-three-year-old resident of Salisbury, Connecticut, asked the town's board of selectmen to allow him to vote as a Whig in a hotly contested local election. The request raised a flurry of objections from the opposition party, for a reason that must be rare in the annals of American democracy: it was said that Suydam was "more female than male," and thus (since only men had the right to vote) should not be allowed to cast a ballot. The selectmen brought in a physician, one William James Barry, to examine Suydam and settle the matter. Presumably upon encountering a phallus and testicles, the good doctor declared the prospective voter male. With Suydam safely in their

perform in myriad ways. The Bem Index actually confronts the sorts of gendered assumptions about men and masculinity that are reinforced through cultural myths, media, and everyday pop culture.

Of course, none of this is to insist that men and women are exactly the same. Rather, the real questions are why binary gender standards are so strictly enforced and why gender distinctions still come at a price—such as lower wages for women, or fewer opportunities for men to nurture and parent. Why is our culture so heavily invested in policing and enforcing particular types of behaviors and prohibiting others? Why are traits that are associated with men or masculinity (e.g., logical reasoning, autonomy) considered better, more valuable, and more worthwhile than traits associated with women or femininity *column the Whigs won the election by a majority of one.*

A few days later, however, Barry discovered that Suydam menstruated regularly and had a vaginal opening. . . . No one has yet discovered whether Sudyam lost the right to vote. . . .

European and American culture is deeply devoted to the idea that there are only two sexes. Even our language refuses other possibilities: thus to write about Levi Suydam . . . I have had to invent conventions— s/he and his/her—to denote individuals who are clearly neither/both male and female or who are, perhaps, both at once. . . . Whether one falls into the category of man or woman matters in concrete ways. For Suydam—and still today for women in some parts of the world—it meant the right to vote. It might mean being subject to the military draft and to various laws concerning the family and marriage. . . .

But if the state and the legal system has an interest in maintaining only two sexes, our collective biological bodies do not. While male and female stand on the extreme ends of a biological continuum, there are many other bodies, bodies such as Suydam's that evidently mix together anatomical components conventionally attributed to both males and fe-males. The implications of my argument for a sexual continuum are pro-found. If nature really offers us more than two sexes, then it follows that our current notions of masculinity and femininity are cultural conceits. Reconceptualizing the category of "sex" challenges cherished aspects of European and American social organization.

(e.g., emotion, interaction, relational reasoning)? These are political arguments—not biological ones—and they affect who gets access to the resources and rewards of our culture.

Morphing Biological Males into Men

In 1949, French existential philosopher Simone de Beauvoir famously wrote in *The Second Sex*, "Woman is made, not born." We can borrow from de Beauvoir to say also that man is made, not born. Antiviolence activist Jackson Katz explains that if we can understand masculinity and gender as fluid, and if we can see certain outcomes of gender socialization (e.g., violent behavior), then we can change the institutional arrangements that encourage, support, and prop up these behaviors.

In an *Atlantis* journal article, Josep M. Armengol points out that "this gendering process—the transformation of biological males into socially interacting men—is a central experience for men," just as it is for women. The biological condition of a boy's birth is only one aspect of his *becoming* a man. Pivotal points through the course of a lifetime create masculine identities. We've already seen the ideological impact that pastel colors such as pink and blue carry with them. Institutions such as kindergarten, Boy Scouts, sports teams, fraternities, advertising, pornography, prostitution, gangs, the sex industry, and the military teach us about masculinity and how guys are supposed to act to be considered "real men."

Men are under constant scrutiny by other men to measure up. Approval among guys involves organizing mainstream U.S. masculinity as a competition to rank as *not* feminine, *not* gay, *not* afraid. All that aggressively stylized and sweaty shoving in the pit at a punk show? Guys who jump in are taking part in homosocial bonding, connecting with each other nonsexually. The same goes for masculine solidarity in hip-hop or the huddle before a football game. When groups of guys catcall a girl, it has little to do with believing that she'll turn around and have sex with them. It's actually about guys performing for other guys. In this instance, guys are bonding with each other using sexist means. Similarly, calling someone a "faggot" has little to do with the targeted person's sexuality. It's about reinforcing masculinity by holding contempt for anyone who seems feminine or untough.

Michael Kimmel has a standing bet that he can walk onto any playground in America where six-year-old boys are happily playing and provoke a fight simply by asking, "Who's a sissy around here?" "One of two things is likely to happen," Kimmel writes.

> *One boy will accuse another of being a sissy, to which that boy will respond that he is not a sissy, that the first boy is. They may have to fight it out to see who's lying. Or a whole group of boys will surround one boy and all shout, "He is! He is!" That boy will either burst into tears and run home*

crying, disgraced, or he will have to take on several boys at once, to prove that he's not a sissy. (And what will his father or older brothers tell him if he chooses to run home crying?) It will be some time before he regains any sense of self-respect.

Mainstream gender lessons for and about boys tend to promote a model of dominant—or hegemonic—masculinity. C. J. Pascoe notes that sexuality is one area in which young men experience particular pressure. Asserting sexual dominance, she writes, is somewhat paradoxical. The high school guys she observed while researching her book talked a big talk about who "wanted" them and who they "did." But these stories about "girl-getting rituals" were less about sexual desire and actually more about, as Pascoe writes, "proving their capacity to exercise control on the world around them, primarily through women's bodies."

With the recent surge in popularity of Viagra, the little blue pill has emerged as a potent way for understanding masculinity as essentially about virility. Viagra creates a metaphor suggesting the male body is like a machine. If it's broken, masculinity can be fixed or regained. This obviously presumes a corporeal masculinity, with its source in the penis. The "Viagra Model" of masculinity also presumes that sexual pleasure is about penetrability and hardness—concepts that are as much ideological visions of masculinity as they are about physiology. In the age of Viagra, writes Meika Loe in "Fixing Broken Masculinity: Viagra as a Technology for the Production of Gender and Sexuality," most medical practitioners and consumers "agree that loss of erectile function appears to be synonymous with loss of manhood." Viagra's emphasis on erectile function also reinforces assumptions that sex equals heterosexual intercourse. We might ask what it means symbolically now that Viagra is promoted for daily use, as a preventive measure, and for nighttime to facilitate nocturnal erections.

Messages about masculinity also involve a huge preoccupation with men's physiques. The media besieges guys with images of muscular male bodies. The message guys get from the time they're little boys is that

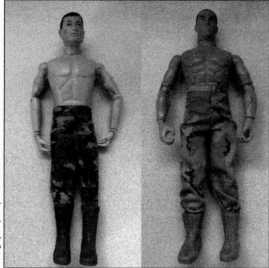

Between the 1960s and the beginning of the twenty-first century, GI Joe's biceps and chest grew disproportionately large compared to the rest of his body.

a "real man" is big and muscular. We have only to look at the evolution of GI Joe through time to see how powerful this message is. Health expert Betty Holmes reports that a human version of GI Joe would be five feet, ten inches tall. This height has remained about the same since the 1960s. What's different, though, is GI Joe's physique: By 2001, the circumference of GI Joe's biceps (in human proportion) grew from an estimated twelve inches to about twenty-seven inches; chest measurements increased dramatically from about forty-four to fifty-five inches during the same period.

Pop culture is a powerful source of the stories we are taught about masculinity. Katz argues that males who feel powerless in the broader society—particularly men of color and working-class white men—often turn to their own bodies as a source of power. That explains why we tend to associate sports such as boxing and basketball, or jobs such as construction and street-level drug dealing, with poor men or men of color. Wealthier, privileged (and often white) men have access to economic, social, and political forms of power that do not require this kind of physical posturing. Men with privilege have additional options.

Pop culture media are more than happy to reinforce this image of men—especially working-class men and men of color—as hard, hyperaggressive, or criminal. Authors Natalie Hopkinson and Natalie

Y. Moore write in their book *Deconstructing Tyrone: A New Look at Black Masculinity in the Hip-Hop Generation* that black males, for example, "make up about six percent of the U.S. population, yet they loom colossal in their constructions as broadcast by media all over the world via sports, crime, and entertainment. In mass media, stereotypical portrayals of ethnic groups have been a tried-and-true shortcut to character development."

According to Byron Hurt, director of the acclaimed film *Hip-Hop: Beyond Beats and Rhymes*, if men do not live up to the ideals of aggressive masculinity, guys risk getting ridiculed for not being man enough. When guys refuse to act out this aggressive version of masculinity, Hurt explains, they risk getting called names such as "soft, weak, pussy, and faggot." Mainstream hip-hop repeatedly reinforces these messages about aggressive masculinity and what it means to be a man. In American culture, being "a real man" is equated with "being hard." Not showing any weakness or emotion is a crucial aspect of being hard and therefore considered "manly." According to Hurt, oftentimes male hip-hop artists feel as if they have to project an image of themselves as thugs, "even if that doesn't reflect who they really are, or who they really want to be." As a result, Hurt says, "this need to conform to the narrow definition of manhood in hip-hop is a trap for men, boxing them into a restricted, unhealthy style of manhood and masculinity."

In *Taking the Field: Men, Women, and Sports,* Michael Messner explains how sport often encourages men to take on the stereotypes of dominant masculinity. One way this is accomplished is by establishing masculinity in opposition to—or not like—gay men or women. Melding dominant masculinity with homophobia and misogyny is reinforced when words such as "faggot," "pussy," and "woman" are used as insults by male athletes, and even by coaches who want their players to be more aggressive.

Sports culture places a powerful emphasis on winning, not being weak, and not having your goal penetrated by the opposing team. For an athlete, these messages about what it means to be a guy are part of a competitive package in which the male athletic body becomes a weapon to fend off other people and forcefully keep them off his turf. This aggression can be translated off the field as violence. For instance, data show that male college athletes are more likely to be violent than other college males. This tells us that sports play a strong role in constructing gender in ways that combine masculinity with dominance and aggression. Messner argues that sports are one institutionalized way "in which boys and men learn and are often rewarded for disciplining their own bodies, attitudes, and feelings within a logic of violence," which can be focused against themselves, other men, or women. Yet again, these attitudes are not innate or unchanging.

Escape from the Man Box

The Man Box is a conceptual framework developed by violence-prevention educators Allan Creighton and Paul Kivel for understanding the dominant standards and norms of masculinity. These boundaries and limitations of dominant masculinity include traits or stereotypes that are familiar to us: Boys and men don't cry; they are tough, big, aggressive; they enjoy competitive sports; they're sexual and powerful. Outside of the Man Box is where we put qualities not associated with mainstream masculinity, such as creativity, kindness, sensitivity, gentleness, and attentiveness. These are human qualities, but if judged against the norms portrayed and perpetuated by mainstream culture, they're generally traits that would cause men to perceive other men as weak. They are also the qualities we tend to associate with femininity. The Man Box constructs masculinity in opposition to femininity, and the traits inside the Man Box tend to be more highly valued than those outside of it. (The national organization A Call to Men points out that in the space beyond the Man Box is where we often find the dancers, poets, writers, and artists.)

The rules of the Man Box make it seem as if all guys are tough, have lots of sex (or say they do), drink with their buddies, and step up and unequivocally take charge. Yet there's a paradox: Nobody

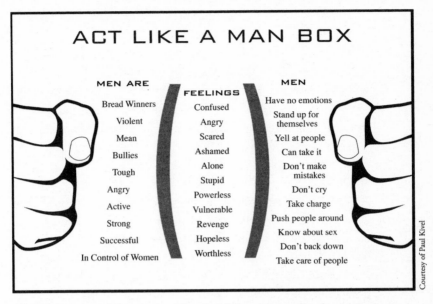

ACT LIKE A MAN BOX

MEN ARE

Bread Winners
Violent
Mean
Bullies
Tough
Angry
Active
Strong
Successful
In Control of Women

FEELINGS

Confused
Angry
Scared
Ashamed
Alone
Stupid
Powerless
Vulnerable
Revenge
Hopeless
Worthless

MEN

Have no emotions
Stand up for themselves
Yell at people
Can take it
Don't make mistakes
Don't cry
Take charge
Push people around
Know about sex
Don't back down
Take care of people

Courtesy of Paul Kivel

The Man Box provides a conceptual framework for understanding how assumptions about masculinity limit the "acceptable" roles, emotions, and behaviors for men.

can really front like this *all the time*. But instead of acknowledging the diversity and complexity of masculinity, pop culture has recently given us a version of manhood that revels in escape. Movies and TV shows in the "failure-to-launch" genre, such as *Superbad*, *The Simpsons*, *Pineapple Express*, *The 40-Year-Old Virgin*, *Knocked Up*, and *Zack and Miri Make a Porno* portray men languishing in a perpetual adolescent state without tons of responsibility.

Journalist Lakshmi Chaudhry, writing for *In These Times*, notes that "commercials for cell phones, fast food, beer and deodorants offer up an infantilized version of masculinity that has become ubiquitous. . . . A recent cell phone ad, for example, features a guy who responds to being dumped by his girlfriend—because 'you're never going to grow up'—by playing, on his cell phone, an '80s pop song that tells her to get lost." This image is a corporate executive's dream customer, says Chaudhry: "a man-boy who is more likely to remain faithful to their product than to his [partner]." The 1950s image of the benevolent patriarch, Chaudhry writes, "has been replaced by an adult teenager who spends his time sneaking off to hang out with the boys, eyeing the hot chick over his wife's shoulder, or buying cool new toys." If we are to believe these sorts of ads, guys can't be trusted with the simplest domestic tasks. We're supposed to believe that guys are so innocently—even humorously—incompetent that they can't be trusted "cooking dinner for the kids or shopping for groceries." (The role of women in these setups, says David Denby of the *New Yorker*, is to tolerate men's antics and to make the men grow up.)

Michael Kimmel reveals the hidden world of what he calls "guyland" in his groundbreaking book by the same name. According to Kimmel, guyland is the social environment that every boy navigates on his way to adulthood. Entertainment, for example, has always been a fun version of escaping from everyday life. What's astounding, Kimmel notes, is the level of dedication, time, and money that guys today exhibit. Escape from daily life often becomes guys' top priority. (X-Box or *World of Warcraft*, anyone?) So is it any wonder, Kimmel asks, that guys on their way to manhood so closely resemble boys?

These slacker assumptions are at odds with the take-charge version of dominant masculinity that's also imposed on men. These images present competing cultural messages to boys and men to take on a stoic hypermasculine pose *and* remain eternally irresponsible, coyly helpless, childlike "kidults." Both versions of masculinity are so extreme and unrealistic, and neither serves men and boys well. Guys are also told that they have power over others. But while men as a group have power over women, many men lack power in other areas of their lives.

Men are both powerful *and* powerless. In fact, guys can sometimes feel really powerless, says Rocco Capraro in his article, "Why College Men Drink: Alcohol, Adventure and the Paradox of Masculinity." Race, class, nation of origin, sexual orientation, and other identity factors further complicate this experience of relative powerlessness. Men make up the "rules of manhood." But not all men are equal.

And the sad irony is that while men's social power is the source of individual privilege, it's also the source of individual pain and alienation. Fitting into a box, feeling restricted, experiencing pressure to perform or to provide can take a heavy toll. Women have a role in this and, as bell hooks writes, as long as they continue to fall for the bad boy, women will remain complicit in upholding these rigid rules of hypermasculine manhood.

Prescriptive messages about masculinity—mixed as they sometimes are—can create shame and even depression in men. These messages can present a real danger when they limit guys' options for exploring what they want to do and who they want to be. When men attempt to live up to prescribed roles, they can experience discomfort that comes from both conforming and not conforming to these roles. Capraro points out that if guys fail to live up to cultural and peer group standards they've internalized, the resulting discomfort (or role strain) is experienced specifically as shame. The core of this shame is a painful self-judgment. Shame can be a catalyst for transformative decisions about behavior. But often for men, shame is deeply repugnant, Capraro says. Because shame is so antithetical to the expectations of masculinity in the first place, men are less likely to transform shame into positive avenues for self-realization.

Michael Kimmel explains that fear and shame are linked: Men become afraid that other guys will find out that on the inside, they're actually scared of not measuring up, of being emasculated. Not measuring up would make us not real men, Kimmel says. Shame is related to fear—that is, "fear of shame" and "shame of fear." A vicious cycle. As Michael Kimmel puts it, fear and shame are at the center of men's identity.

To handle this, Kimmel says, men become distanced from anything associated with the feminine (mothers, feelings, nurturing, intimacy, vulnerability). In other words, men and boys internalize male gender roles to avoid shame. They also learn through this process that dependency needs are shameful. Another vicious cycle. Depression also becomes a risk for men especially because of dissociation from feelings and related destructive behavior.

And if dissociative behavior is the only option available to men to transform uncomfortable feelings, and it's a limited option at that, then men learn to manage shame, depression, and fear in particularly harmful ways, especially through drinking. Heavy or binge drinking is one way that men may act out these emotions. It's socially sanctioned. Women might cry or eat chocolate. That's what women are "allowed" to do. Men are "allowed" to drink.

In every study of college drinking, men drink more than women. Women and men report drinking to be social. But men are more likely to report that they drink to escape and that they drink to get drunk. And yet while men might drink to feel powerful (or just tanked), the paradox is that drinking decreases men's power, particularly through the loss of control of emotion, health, and basic motor functions.

There are, however, other ways for men to deal with the gap between the cultural myths about masculinity that surround them every day and the realities of who they are and how they choose to live their lives. Mainstream American culture might fetishize a version of masculinity that objectifies women and is unable to connect intimately with another person, yet research reveals that American men today do more work at home than their fathers did, and they are happy doing it. In a report from the Radcliffe Public Policy Center, Leslie G. Cintron found that 71 percent of men between twenty-one and thirty-nine years old were willing to give up pay and promotions if it meant they could have more time to spend with their families. Single men are beginning to explore options in surrogacy and adoption in order to become fathers.

Mainstream culture gives men all sorts of mixed and negative messages about masculinity, but research tells us that men's lives don't really conform with the messages they're shown. "College guys believe that 80 percent of their friends are getting laid each weekend," reports Tony Dokoupil in a 2008 *Newsweek* article about how "Peter Pans aren't as happy as they seem." Despite bravado, sexual posturing, or assumptions about what their friends are doing between the sheets, the actual number of eighteen- to twenty-two-year-old guys hooking up is closer to 10 percent. After college, "the percentages merely get worse," Michael Kimmel says. And the fact is, men seem to do well in monogamous relationships. A slew of recent studies suggest that

On Being a Man

The violence of men. It appears so senseless, so random, but if we look deeply at the culture, at the spiritual losses and the capitalist relations that place property rights over human rights, material goods over spirituality, then the violence begins to make a lot of sense . . . [but] no man can find his essence, can get a hold of his own true self, as long as he participates, whether willfully or not, in a world that is predicated on man's power over woman.

—Luis J. Rodriguez, "On Macho"

Un hombre que es macho is not hypermasculine or aggressive, and he does not disrespect or denigrate women. Machos, according to the positive view, adhere to a code of ethics that stresses humility, honor, respect of oneself and others, and courage. What may be most significant in this second view is that being "macho" is not manifested by such outward qualities as physical strength and virility but by such inner qualities as personal integrity, commitment, loyalty, and, most importantly, strength of character.

—Alfredo Mirandé, *Hombres y Machos: Masculinity and Latino Culture*

The ultimate measure of a man is not where he stands in moments of comfort and convenience, but where he stands at times of challenge and controversy.

—Martin Luther King Jr., *Strength to Love*

Manliness consists not in bluff, bravado, or lordliness. It consists in daring to do the right [thing] and facing consequences whether it is in matters social, political, or other. It consists in deeds, not in words.

—Mahatma Gandhi

coupled men "are happier, more sexually satisfied and less likely to end up in the emergency room" than their uncoupled counterparts, Dokoupil writes. The sexual rhetoric-reality gap is similar to the gap between locker room talk and real-guy talk. The reputation is that guys' locker-room talk is full of bawdy bravado, but Michael Messner says most guy talk actually involves "quiet, dyadic discussions of relationships, fears, and doubts," and hopes, dreams, and desires.

Our ideas about masculinity are propped up by all sorts of cultural sources such as religion, family, schools, fairytales, sports heroes, science, and everyday myths that are so common that they become invisible to us. Yet even though the politics of masculinity are so often invisible to us, gender politics are everywhere. When we make gender visible, then we can start talking about the possibilities of positive masculinity. The question is what would that version of masculinity look like? And how would we make it happen?

The good news is that there are infinite possibilities for creating positive masculinity. Being a real man doesn't have to mean setting oneself up in binary opposition to femininity. Masculinity doesn't have to hinge on power and control over others. Real masculinity can involve valuing a wide range of emotions, experiences, preferences, desires, and accomplishments in all people.

Chapter 4

Gender Advantage:
Checking In on Masculine Privilege

MASCULINE PRIVILEGE IS THE IDEA THAT society confers certain unearned advantages on men simply because they are male. Masculine privilege operates in everyday events. Sometimes it's really obvious, as in the fact that Congress remains overwhelmingly male. But masculine privilege also flies under the radar. Institutional practices and ideological beliefs about masculine superiority seem so normal or natural that we've learned not to notice when a man's opinion is taken more seriously than a woman's or that calling a boy a "girl" is considered an insult.

Exposing invisible patterns and practices allows us to think critically about the links between gender privilege and sexism. One way masculine privilege operates is in how men (and women) are taught to see sexism as "individual acts of meanness," says feminist scholar Peggy McIntosh. What's really going on, though, is that sexism is supported by invisible systems that perpetuate and maintain dominance for men *as a group*.

This process is similar to how racism and white skin privilege work, McIntosh comments in her essay "White Privilege: Unpacking the Invisible Knapsack." As a white woman McIntosh can turn on the TV or look at the front page of the newspaper and assume she'll see people of her race widely represented. Jewel Woods draws parallels with his status as a man; he writes in "The Black Male Privileges Checklist" that as a man he can assume that his financial success or popularity as an athlete will not be associated with his looks. If he wants to "sow some wild oats," he won't be judged for it. Friends might even encourage him. Woods also notes that privilege looks different for men of color than it does for white men. "Examining black male privilege," Woods writes, "offers black men and boys an opportunity to go beyond old arguments of 'personal responsibility' or 'blaming the man' to gain a deeper level of insight into how issues of class and race are influenced by gender."

Masculine privilege and its benefits are real, but they're often hard to see. They go unrecognized because they're so common. The ideological, structural, and institutional factors of masculine privilege tend to remain invisible. And men tend to be unaware of their own privileges as men.

Masculine privilege includes individual actions, but it exists on a larger scale as well. So even if a man says, "Well, I'm not sexist. I'm not like *that*," masculine privilege isn't so easy to shrug off. In general, men more easily than women walk through the world with a sense of status and cultural legitimacy that isn't necessarily conscious or articulated. And it's not necessarily something that men *ask* for. Men are conferred status and legitimacy by a culture with a long history of doing so. Masculine privilege functions on a macro level through the ways our institutional and cultural systems are systemically structured.

For instance, antisexist author Hank Shaw reports in "It's Time for Guys to Put an End to This" that 85 percent of reported rapes in the United States end up with no conviction by the courts. Almost 90 percent of reported rapes result in no jail time. One question is why there are so many rapes in the first place—to the tune of 876,000 a year, by some estimates. (The American Medical Association counts seven hundred thousand and according to the Rape, Abuse and Incest National Network, 60 percent of sexual assaults are still not reported to the police.) "No matter which figure you choose," says Shaw, "it's WAY TOO MUCH." Shaw connects the dots between masculine privilege, violence, and institutionalized patterns of power imbalances. One possible reason there are so many sexual assaults perpetrated by men,

Shaw writes, is that "these guys think they have the right to sex, even though it's not in the Constitution. They also think their right to sex is greater than the right of a woman to say 'NO!' Which is another way of saying this: 'Men are more important than women. So we get to make the rules,'" says Shaw.

These sorts of beliefs come from masculinist ideologies of privilege. These ideologies are models for exerting power over others—and then ignoring this process, or choosing to look the other way. Some people deflect attention from masculine privilege by arguing that men are just as affected by assault as women, or that women actually have more power because they can falsely accuse men of rape. Tragically, it's true that more than one hundred thousand boys and men are raped every year, according to Shaw. But 90 percent of all rape victims or survivors are women, and 60 percent are girls under the age of eighteen. The rapists are overwhelmingly grown men. Furthermore, the National Coalition Against Violent Athletes reports on its website that, according to the FBI, "More people falsely report their own death than file a false report alleging sexual assault."

Understanding power and privilege means taking seriously not only gender dynamics but also issues of race, class, ethnicity, age, ability, sexual orientation, and nation of origin. This means knowing, for instance, that black people comprise 13 percent of the national population but 30 percent of those arrested, according to the nonprofit group Human Rights Watch. This disparity isn't necessarily caused entirely by racism among cops—but that doesn't mean racism doesn't exist. Like sexism, racism is more complicated than that, which is exactly what makes it so powerful. Researchers believe, for example, that racial disparities in the criminal justice system result from "indirect" forms of discrimination such as poverty, lack of educational opportunities, and increased police scrutiny in particular neighborhoods. These institutionalized disadvantages are "compounded throughout the criminal justice processing system," reports Human Rights Watch.

Being a member of any dominant group includes the ability to not notice one's privilege. So white skin privilege can mean driving through a neighborhood without thinking about race and whether the police are going to pull you over. White privilege can mean the luxury of walking into a room without thinking about the color of your skin because white people don't usually think about their skin tone unless they're the only white person in the room. Similarly, paying attention to the sex/gender of your sexual partners isn't something people generally do if they're straight.

And the same thing is true for men. Men don't usually wake up in the morning and think about their privilege or even the fact of being male. The unexamined assumptions and the ongoing invisibilities of gender privilege make masculine privilege powerful because it goes underground. It enables men to be unself-conscious about privilege and status. And that's the privilege: *not* having to think about one's gendered identity. In other words, the concept of masculine privilege includes the luxury of not having to notice one's gender.

Women are often acutely aware of being gendered female as they make their way through everyday experiences in the world. Not paying attention to masculinity might mean walking to your car at night *without* thinking about personal safety or the possibility of sexual assault. Women often hold their keys at the ready, walk in pairs, or remain hypervigilant about their surroundings in ways that often simply don't occur to men. Because girls are raised knowing they will be judged on how they look, women are intensely aware of their image from head to toe. Men may not give a second thought to what they're wearing. Looking good can matter for everyone, but the social stakes for men are not as high if they look sloppy, unattractive, skinny, or fat. And what if a woman feels cranky one day? What if she's deep in thought, or she just doesn't feel like smiling? Women are used to being told by total strangers to smile (read: Be more friendly and less ornery). Men are rarely—if ever—told to smile. Men are not required to be socially accessible. Men don't generally get accused of PMS-ing (again, read: not being nice enough). Being acutely aware of one's gender in this way is something men rarely experience.

Walk a Mile in Her Shoes: The International Men's March to Stop Rape, Sexual Assault, and Gender Violence provides men an opportunity to put themselves in the shoes of women and imagine what it's like to routinely face the threat of violence. Here, participants wear high-heeled shoes during a 2008 march in Laramie, Wyoming.

Masculine privilege can be a touchy issue for a lot of us to read about or discuss. These conversations can feel threatening. Men might feel defensive; they might feel as if they're being accused of being sexist. Women might think men are being singled out for attack and want to stand up for them. But we can't adequately address sexism without discussing masculine privilege. Sidestepping the subject is like trying to eradicate racism without ever mentioning white privilege. This subject can provoke discomfort, but talking about masculine privilege is a crucial conversation. It is a subject that's important to investigate.

The point of conversations about power and privilege is not simply to declare that unearned privilege is always bad. Those of us who have privilege shouldn't just sit around feeling guilty about it (and then pat ourselves on the backs for knowing enough about sexism and racism to feel guilty in the first place). The impact of unearned privilege depends on what we *do* with it. Success and change lie in figuring out how privilege—whether based on gender, race, class, sexual orientation, religion, or any other aspect of identity—can be relinquished or used for positive change.

Hey, What's in That Guy's Knapsack?

Masculine privilege lends men access to power, which has a serious impact on gender equality. Some forms of injustice, such as sexual assault or pay inequity, are obvious and concrete. Other instances of bias are damaging precisely because they're so hard to pinpoint. Masculine privilege is buttressed by a sexism that runs so deep through our collective psyches that, as Shulamith Firestone suggests, biased sex and gender divisions are practically invisible. These invisible practices easily go unnoticed until somebody calls them out.

When little boys are encouraged to be more active or are allowed to get dirtier than girls when they play, there is subtle yet profound gender construction at hand in which boys learn to exercise a greater range of motion and physicality. Most pronouns used for God are masculine (His, Him, Father), and most visual images for God are male. The pronoun "guys" may, without question, refer to a group of both men and women, but referring to that same group as "girls" is an unacceptable alternative.

Men can walk relatively freely through the world without fear of sexual harassment and rape (unless they are young boys, are gay, are incarcerated, or visibly deviate from gender norms). Men can assume people will listen when they talk, and they don't generally struggle to make their voices heard (although this may not necessarily be true in a mixed-race group of men). Men don't usually have to worry that if they are aggressive or opinionated they will be condemned or called a "bitch."

If you can show up for class in jeans and a T-shirt and feel pretty sure you won't be criticized for not wearing makeup, chances are you are the recipient of masculine privilege. Same goes if you are expected to spend little money on beauty and hygiene products. (Just for kicks, ask your female and male friends how many products they used this morning before they left their houses. Then do the math and figure out how much money men saved. These savings are the result of gendered beauty and consumer expectations.) Because we are surrounded by examples of gender privilege and bias every day, we become used to them. If we notice it at all, masculine privilege can seem normal or natural.

Feminist and antiviolence activist Ben Atherton-Zeman comments, "Heterosexual men listen to songs all about how our gender is the victim of female manipulation and heartbreak. But in reality, my gender exists with a privilege that's invisible. We're safer on the streets, safer at work, safer in our homes. We make more money than women do, see our faces more on television, and are represented by leaders that look like us."

Men can take for granted that they're the norm, the standard bearers. Guys—especially straight, white, able-bodied guys—can be pretty sure that when they see the front page of the newspaper, flip through the sports section, or meet their tenured physics professor, the faces they see will look a lot like their own. And when those faces don't—as when the doctor, dentist, or plumber turns out to be a woman—it might be a big surprise. The fact that people still specify "female" doctor but don't spell out "male" doctor is evidence that a male norm is still in play. Books, magazines, college campuses, and television shows still tend to make universal assumptions that words such as "mankind," "chairman," "policeman," or "freshman" refer to everyone.

What we think of as regular or neutral is often based on the assumption of a male standard. For most professional sports teams, the men's league is the presumed norm and the women's is the exception. The NBA is men's basketball, but women's pro-ball is singled out as the WNBA. Colors that are thought of as gender neutral, such as blue and green, are associated with boys. Clothing that is thought of as gender neutral is associated with men (pants, slacks, suits, etc.) not women (skirts, stockings, dresses, etc.).

Masculine privilege means guys can turn on the radio or watch music videos knowing it's unlikely they will encounter lyrics or visual images that refer to them in sexually degrading or objectifying ways.

The Unearned Benefits of Being Male

In Peggy McIntosh's 1988 essay on privilege, she wrote, "I have begun in an untutored way to ask what it is like to have white privilege. I have come to see white privilege as an invisible package of unearned assets that I can count on cashing in each day, but about which I was 'meant' to remain oblivious. White privilege is like an invisible weightless knapsack of special provisions, maps, passports, codebooks, visas, clothes, tools, and blank checks."

McIntosh's important insight provided the groundwork for men such as Paul Kivel, Jewel Woods, and Barry Deutsch, who have borrowed her concept and created similar lists about male privilege.

Do you benefit from unearned privileges because you are male? How many of the following can you check off? Some examples will be mediated by experiences of class, race, nation of origin, religion, and sexual orientation. These aspects of privilege are important issues to consider and discuss.

1. I can be pretty sure that when I walk down the street, nobody will yell at me about my body or tell me what they want to do to me sexually.
2. My forefathers, including my father, had more opportunities to advance themselves economically than my foremothers.
3. When I learn about the civil rights and Black Power movements, most of the leaders that I learn about are men.
4. If I choose not to have children, nobody will question my masculinity.
5. No one will think I'm selfish if I have children and a career.
6. In school, boys' sports were given more attention than girls' sports. There were cheerleaders for boys' teams, but none for the girls.
7. At work, I can be fairly sure that I won't be sexually harassed.
8. If I have sex with a lot of women, it's unlikely that I'll be called a chickenhead, slut, or a ho.
9. I will not be expected to attend a "purity ball" to celebrate virginity until marriage.
10. I can be pretty sure that when I talk in groups or in public, people

will listen to what I'm saying and they will believe I know what I'm talking about.

11. I've gotten work, a job interview, job training, or an internship through personal connections with men.

12. I can be reasonably assured that in my intimate relationships and everyday life I am unlikely to be the victim of domestic violence or sexual assault.

13. I generally feel safe when walking to my car by myself at night, hiking alone in the woods or the mountains, or walking on the beach.

14. I can turn on the TV or open the newspaper and expect to see people of my sex represented, including political and business leaders, top athletes, movie stars, and experts. My elected representatives are mostly people of my own sex.

15. When I have medical procedures, take prescribed medicines, or receive other health treatments, I can assume they were tested and proven safe on people of my own sex.

16. I have heard men belittle women's abilities, women's writing or music, women's intelligence, or physical strength, or make other comments about women being inferior to men—especially if there are no women are in the room when they say it.

17. I know that if I want to, I can pay money to have sex with women or to watch them dance with their clothes off.

18. I have easy access to sexually revealing images of women on the Internet and in books and movies.

19. I can assume that I'll do less of the housecleaning, cooking, childcare, washing, or other caregiving than the women in my family do.

20. I can dress how I want, without people assuming I want to have sex with them.

21. When I have sex, I don't have to worry about pregnancy if I don't feel like it.

22. I don't need to think about sexism every day. I have the privilege of not having to think about my privilege.

This sidebar draws on and was adapted from the works of Peggy McIntosh, Paul Kivel, Jewel Woods, and Barry Deutsch.

The film *Dreamworlds 3*, a groundbreaking movie about music videos and the stories they tell about women and girls, convincingly describes how pop culture media send powerful messages about men's sexual access to women's bodies. Music videos are a central part of our pop culture, and they routinely portray women's bodies in hypersexualized, objectified ways. Yet if we are not taught media literacy tools, we tend to see these images as "just entertainment" instead of understanding that music videos also reveal significant messages about sexuality and relations between women and men.

When it comes to home and family life, many men report wanting to spend more time with their children. But in actual practice, it is frequently assumed that women, not men, will interrupt their careers to raise families. As feminist blogger Barry Deutsch puts it in "Unpacking Men's Invisible Knapsack," "If I have children with a wife or girlfriend, and it turns out that one of us needs to make career sacrifices to raise the kids, chances are we'll both assume the career sacrificed should be hers." Often this decision seems rational because the male partner is already earning more money. Yet this is actually an example of how privilege begets more privilege. That's not to say that career or money automatically equals privilege, but that *options, choices,* and *earnings potential* are all hallmarks of privilege.

When it comes to marriage practices, the vast majority of men don't change their last names after getting married. It simply might not cross men's minds, or they might laugh at the mere suggestion. While taking a woman's surname after marriage might seem weird, U.S. institutional structures reinforce and maintain the assumption that men will keep their own names. Steve Friess, writing for *USA Today*, reports that ingrained patriarchal traditions have been slowly challenged by a few men who have taken their wives' last names. Yet as of 2007 more than forty states actually prevented a man who wants "to alter his name after his wedding to do so without going through the laborious, frequently expensive legal process set out by the courts for any name change." In these states, there wasn't even an option on the marriage license application for the groom to choose the bride's name.

The American Civil Liberties Union takes this issue seriously. In 2006, Michael Buday elected to use the last name of his new wife, Diana Bijon. After months of frustration and discovering that it would take a $350 fee, court appearances, a public announcement, and mounds of paperwork to change his driver's license (hoops that women don't jump through), Buday took his case to the ACLU of Southern California. Jill Serjeant reports for Reuters that California state law now guarantees "the rights of both married couples and registered domestic partners to choose whichever last name they prefer on their marriage and driving licenses." Mark Rosenbaum, legal director of the Southern California chapter of the ACLU, comments that this new law "disposes of the rule in California that the male surname is the marital name to the same trash bin where dowries were once tossed out."

The decision to hyphenate last names might appear to be an egalitarian practice, but it's usually the woman who does this—and it's still considered somewhat unusual when a man joins her. Friess notes that Sam Van Hallgren, the cohost of a movie-review podcast, *Filmspotting*, had to placate his listeners who were caught off guard the first time Van Hallgren introduced himself with his new name. (Van Hallgren was formerly Sam Hallgren until he married Carrie Van Deest and they combined names.) The social risk proved high for Van Hallgren: According to Friess, he "received a scathing note from a longtime listener with a subject line that read, 'Sam, turn in your man card.' The listener asked what 'sissy juice' the host was drinking."

Linguistic Shape-Shifting

Language is one of the key ways that our culture, consciously or not, conceals masculine privilege. Sometimes it's as simple as stating "female" before "doctor," as mentioned above, or using "mankind" to describe humankind. But other times the manipulation of language is more complicated.

Linguistic shape-shifting is what Jackson Katz calls the nearly imperceptible practice of making men, boys, and masculinity disappear through how we use language. Katz explains that this "disappearing act" involves using gender-neutral language to obscure gender-*specific* events such as men's responsibility for violence. "We cannot achieve dramatic reductions in men's violence against women," Katz says, "until we can at least *name* the problem correctly." Tragedies such as the 1998 Jonesboro Massacre, Columbine in 1999, the 1999 gang rapes in Woodstock, the sexual assaults in Central Park during Puerto Rican Day festivities in 2000, the shooting of ten Amish girls in 2006, and the thirty-two murders during the 2007 Virginia Tech rampage were reported as violent attacks, or as "kids killing kids," rather than what they really were—*men's* (and boys') violent assaults.

Katz explains that the way we structure language allows men to slip out of view. For instance, the sentence "Mary is a battered woman" emphasizes a woman's condition and diverts attention away from male violence. This lets men and our society collectively off the hook from taking a cold hard look at gendered violence. In his book *The Macho Paradox: Why Some Men Hurt Women and How All Men Can Help*, Katz cites linguist Julia Penelope's work in tracing the transition from male accountability to passive invisibility: 1) John beat Mary. 2) Mary was beaten by John. 3) Mary was beaten. 4) Mary was battered. 5) Mary is a battered woman. By the end not only has "John" disappeared from the equation, but "Mary's" identity is sealed by the status of her victimization.

This linguistic shape-shifting matters because the media frequently use passive descriptions when they report on male violence against women. This passive style reinforces ideas that domestic violence and sexual assault are "women's issues," and men are left out of the picture. "John left the conversation long ago, while Mary evolves into the active victim," Katz explains. "Victim-blaming is very pervasive in our society, because this is how our whole power structure is set up. We start asking why Mary put herself into a position to be beaten by John. If we really want to work on preventing sexual assault and male violence against women, we need to start asking questions about John, not Mary," Katz says. In other words, we need to shift the paradigm at the cultural level and start treating domestic violence and assault as men's issues.

In "The Grammar of Male Violence," Jennie Ruby also describes how language focuses on women as victims but not on the role of men as perpetrators. Crime reports are written in the passive voice. "The result is that the gender of the victim is clearly stated," Ruby writes, "but the gender of the perpetrator is completely hidden: 'A woman was raped' rather than 'A man raped a woman' or 'A man raped someone,' or even 'An unknown male assailant raped a person.'" These passive oversights of language are at the core of masculine privilege: the privilege not to have to notice privilege, and the privilege of disappearing from accountability. What results is that men can collectively stay in the same place and the cultural systems of masculine privilege remain unexamined. This limits society's ability to effectively address important issues of power and privilege, safety and liberty. The focus remains on helping women escape violence rather than on reducing violent behavior in men.

A similar process is at work in the way the news media report on reproductive politics. Recent headlines in major newspapers, on websites, and in magazines announced an "epidemic" of teen pregnancy and a rising concern about the rate of sexually transmitted infection among teen girls. So what's the problem with this picture? Don't we care about reproductive issues and the sexual well-being of girls and young women?

We do, of course. But, as Mike Males points out in the *Los Angeles Times*, not only are the sensationalist reports about rising teen pregnancy rates fact-challenged, they also revive a host of pre-1950s-esque sexist misnomers. What's more, this kind of reporting diverts attention away from the complexity of the situation. A large majority of male partners involved in teenage pregnancy are men age twenty and older, Males writes. Instead of criticizing the "high rate of teenage pregnancy" in the United States, it would make sense to say something about the high rate of adult men who are impregnating teen girls.

The same goes for teenage girls who contract conditions such as HPV, chlamydia, or HIV/AIDS. The partners responsible for sexually transmitting these infections—partners who are usually male—are removed from the focus of public debate. When it comes to public discussion about teen pregnancy and STIs, men are often erased from the equation. Removing men from public scrutiny once again lets men off the hook and leaves social problems only partially addressed.

Pornography and Privilege

Some people argue that pornography is another way masculine privilege is constructed and reinforced. It's true that pornography certainly highlights women's sexual bodies. But porn doesn't focus *only* on women. Not all pornography is straight or heternormative, but a lot of it is. And men aren't the only ones looking: Women watch porn, too. So how can we know that pornography reinforces male privilege?

The vast majority of pornography depicts sex acts being done *to* women, women being on display for the pleasure of others, women depicted as deriving pleasure primarily by pleasing others. This is not a moral issue; it's a political one. Sex and pleasure are great. Some political theorists such as Herbert Marcuse even argue that sexual pleasure is a form of political liberation. And what consenting adults enjoy sexually or what they do with their bodies is their personal choice. But in *mainstream* porn, the viewer is usually assumed to be male, cruelty or degradation of women plays a central role, and women's bodies exist mostly for men's pleasure. To be blunt, given that face shots, gang bangs, gonzo, and airtight scenes are stock material, we need to start asking some real questions about gender politics and mainstream pornography. The point is not to ban porn or to demonize people who make it or who like to watch it but to understand how porn functions in propping up masculine privilege and influencing our cultural narratives about sexuality.

We live in a culture that is infused with pornographic imagery. Porn and sex work have become models emulated by so much of mainstream life—for example, pole-dancing fitness classes, easy Internet access to porn, porn-peddling banner ads and email spam, porn-infused music videos, and G-strings with cherries and the words "eye candy" marketed to tween girls. With the mainstreaming of pornography melded onto a culture with preexisting gender disparities, we tend to end up with a narrow version of sexual pleasure. Because pornography has a wider reach than it used to, it is fast becoming the primary way that people learn about sexuality and pleasure. Yet in porn we see the same sexual tropes repeated over and over. This gives the misguided impression that pornography provides visions of sexual diversity when it actually offers lots of opportunities to see the same thing. It's like fast food: Coast-to-coast drive-throughs offer lots of chances to get the same hamburger and fries. They don't offer a lot of options in choosing what to eat.

Some might say to all this: Lighten up! Porn is just about getting off. It's just fantasy. Robert Jensen calls this a "definitional dodge"—a bunch of smoke and mirrors. To Jensen, the real issue is how hegemonic masculinity and masculine privilege remain invisible in pornography. Avoiding any frank discussion about pornography by calling it fantasy effectively staves off critique, even preemptively.

The definitional dodge enables us to avoid confronting issues of masculine privilege by claiming that porn is just free expression, says Jensen. The "dodge" usually involves some combination of arguing that porn is all a matter of taste; that what's porn to some is erotica to others; that what's degrading to some is liberating to others; that arguments about pornography are entirely subjective; that we can't precisely define pornography so therefore we can't really say much about it; or, what's the big deal? It's just fantasy.

Arguing that porn is just fantasy is like saying advertising has no effect on our buying habits. Or that news media have no impact on how we understand current events. How could it be true that every other form of mass media has an impact on our habits and collective consciousness, but that porn is "just fantasy"? And even if porn is "just fantasy," then what do these fantasies reveal about the ways in which gender and masculinity are constructed and about how privilege is reinforced and maintained? And what are the consequences of these common cultural tropes?

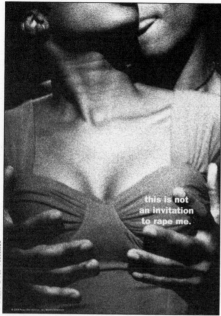

this is not
an invitation
to rape me.

© Peace Over Violence

Peace over Violence (formerly the Los Angeles Commission Against Assault on Women) ran a poster campaign called "This Is Not an Invitation to Rape." The images in the campaign, including this one, attempt to convey that all sexual activity requires the enthusiastic consent of all parties involved.

One study of campus-based sexual assault found that men were sexual aggressors toward more than half of college women interviewed; 47 percent of men who had committed an act that met the legal definition of rape said they expected to engage in a similar assault in the future; 88 percent of men who reported having committed an assault that met the legal definition of rape were adamant that they had not committed rape. Meanwhile, only 27 percent of women who experienced assaults that met the legal definition of rape labeled themselves as rape victims or survivors. Jensen points out that rape and sexual assault are common fodder for entertainment and supply key plot lines in movies, music video, and television. "We live in a culture in which the sex-domination nexus is so tight that victim and victimizer alike often do not recognize the violence in acts that the society has deemed violent enough to be illegal." According to Jensen, the inability to recognize sexual assault—for either perpetrator or survivor—is at the core of what's called a rape culture, and it is propped up by mainstream pornography.

But It Was Just a Joke

Jokes about women's bodies and brains can mask sexism and perpetuate masculine privilege. The problem is that there's a real difference between sexually explicit or erotic humor and jokes that mix sexuality

Gray Rape

"Gray rape" describes fuzzy sexual situations in which it's unclear whether an assault occurred—maybe there was regrettable sex, or people were so wasted that the line between consent and assault seemed unclear. In her popular *Cosmopolitan* magazine article, author Laura Sessions Stepp refers to gray rape as "sex that falls somewhere between consent and denial." Stepp says gray rape is even more confusing than acquaintance rape, or date rape, "because often both parties are unsure of who wanted what."

The action-oriented group Men Can Stop Rape strongly disagrees that there's such a thing as gray rape. The group argues that the term lessens men's accountability and distracts from the real issue, which is whether all parties agreed to have sex with each other. In a poll on its website, the group asks, "Is 'gray rape' society's traditional way of holding men less accountable OR is it a viable result of today's casual hookups, mixed signals, and alcohol (use)?" Discussing these issues and increasing awareness about different forms of sexual assault and what constitutes consent is a form of taking feminist action.

Men Can Stop Rape wants to know which of the following describes what you believe about "gray rape":

- It's just society's traditional way of holding men less accountable (and in turn pointing the finger back at women).
- It's a result of the current equal-opportunity hookup culture.
- It's a result of increased drug and alcohol use that accompanies today's wild partying.
- It's a combination of all the above.

Or maybe you're thinking, "Wait up! There's a heck of a lot more to the issue than this."

with aggression. The former might be funny; the latter create feelings of discomfort and even threat. Often we aren't taught the tools to distinguish between the two.

Jokes that individual men tell women tend to be erotic and clever (such as punch lines that hinge on double entendres). These kinds of jokes are intended to be seductive, professor Peter Lyman explains in "The Fraternal Bond as a Joking Relationship." These sorts of jokes are used by men particularly when they're trying to attract women. But jokes that men tell other men *about* women tend to be sexual and aggressive rather than erotic. They tend to be hostile rather than clever. They tend to be sexist rather than sexual. The purpose seems to be to create homosocial bonding. This is done, however, through reinforcing women as hypersexualized females who can be dominated or denigrated.

Some might find the following jokes funny, innocent, offensive, or rude:

Q: *How do you change a woman's mind?*
A: *Buy her another beer.*

Q: *What is the difference between your job and your wife?*
A: *After twenty years your job still sucks.*

Are these jokes erotic or misogynist? (And how can we tell the difference?) Are they funny *because* they call out the sexism of everyday life? When we hear them, do we laugh or cringe, feel shocked or angry? Or do we pride ourselves on being unshockable and "ironic"? Do we find ourselves laughing even if we don't really think a joke is funny?

Whether women (or men) experience a joke as funny or as intimidating can be a matter of context. If jokes about women are made in an atmosphere of physical intimidation, that becomes a power issue, Lyman writes. And if you're the one on the scene without the power, this can be frightening. It increases men's power and tends to silence women. Sexist jokes themselves are a power issue, whether they are made in an atmosphere of physical intimidation or at the workplace or in an intimate relationship; the jokes themselves, in reinforcing masculine privilege, point out men's power over women.

Jokes can be used to covertly reinforce women's subjugation because jokes ask us to let go of our objections. And if we refuse to let the objections go, we might be called humorless, or we might be accused of being a killjoy. Labels such as these are a quick route to minimizing or dismissing people's concerns. To seal the deal, the seemingly innocent phrase, "Boys will be boys," might be deployed. This again lets men and boys off the hook and clears them of responsibility. As this pattern of dismissing objection and concern is repeated the stakes get higher. Our culture asks us to overlook misogyny whether the issue is jokes that cut down women, sexist DJs on drive-time talk radio, hiring strippers for frat or bachelor parties, sports-related violence, sexual assault at military academies, or expecting access to women's—and even children's—bodies through global sex tourism.

Unequal Privilege

While there is an unearned privilege that's awarded to men simply for being born male, it's a privilege complicated by other aspects of identity. The way activist Atherton-Zeman puts it, "Many of us guys want to deny we have privilege, since we don't especially *feel* privileged. We feel victimized—as working class or poor men, GBTQ men, as men of color, or just as men trying to navigate relationships and the world."

Black, Latino, and Arab men, as well as other men of color, are more closely scrutinized by the criminal justice system. These men experience endemic racism. This means that black men, for instance, have certain status as *men* yet often lack status and privilege as *black* men. The disproportionate numbers of black men imprisoned relative to the total population of black men is one example of discrimination and unequal access to basic rights such as fair and just treatment by the criminal justice system.

Transgender and transsexual individuals also have a complicated relationship to masculine privilege. Author-activist Matt Kailey comments that female-to-male transsexuals are often criticized for transitioning into male privilege. "Sometimes we are accused of transitioning specifically to gain this privilege," Kailey says. "And although many transmen will admit to experiencing newfound privilege, at least superficially, after transition, the bottom line is that we are still transsexuals, one of the least privileged groups in society today. Some transmen, depending on ethnicity, economic level, and several other factors, can enjoy a measure of post-transition male privilege. But when our transsexuality is revealed or discovered, all bets are off."

Younger boys can also experience the effects of relative powerlessness. Systemic abuse of power exists, for instance, when boys are sexually assaulted by grown men. Data provided by Darkness to Light, an organization dedicated to confronting child sexual abuse, indicate that one out of six boys survives sexual abuse by the time he is eighteen years old. More than 60 percent of the time, the perpetrators are men. (Only 10 percent of these pedophiles are strangers, and when girls are assaulted the perpetrator is almost always male.) The expectation that boys don't cry or express hurt contributes to the fact that male childhood abuse continues to be underreported. When society looks the other way or fails to acknowledge male patterns of abuse, it reinforces tacitly sanctioned practices of domination that so deeply affect how we understand our world, our emotions, and our relations with others.

The presence of complex, multilayered patterns of subjugation is why some people have started using the term "kyriarchy" instead of "patriarchy" to describe sociopolitical structures of domination and the abuse of power. As explained by Lisa Factora-Borchers on her blog, *My Ecdysis,* and repeated by Lauren Smith on *Jadedhippy,* patriarchy refers literally to "rule of the father." But all men do not have the same access to power and privilege. *All* men do not dominate *all* women equally, in the same way. Theologian Elisabeth Schüssler Fiorenza coined the term "kyriarchy," which comes from *kyrios,* the Greek word

for "lord" or "master," and *archein*, meaning to rule or dominate."
Schüssler Fiorenza explains that kyriarchy points to how the structures
of domination are intersecting and "multiplicative." This structure
looks like a pyramid of people where a few people are in charge and a
lot of people are at the bottom. It's a system "of ruling and oppression,"
explains Schüssler Fiorenza.

When people talk about the "shifting circles of privilege, power,
and domination—they're [actually] talking about kyriarchy," writes
Factora-Borchers. When you talk about the power a white woman
asserts over a brown man, that's kyriarchy. "When you talk about a
Black man dominating a Brown womyn, that's kyriarchy. It's about . . .
everyone trying to take the role of lord/master within a pyramid."

Clearly, we benefit from creating more precise terms to explain
the complex patterns of privilege and the abuse of power. bell hooks
uses the phrase "white supremacist, capitalist, patriarchy" to describe
these complicated structures of domination. hooks explains that white
supremacist capitalist patriarchy creates and maintains the center and
the margins in society. What she means is that people with power and
access to resources "live" at the center of society. These are the movers
and shakers, the people who get to decide and define what's important
in society. Those at the margins are quite literally *marginalized*. For
instance, a homeowner would be at the center; his or her immigrant
housekeeper would be at the margins.

Yet it's not the case that men *always* have privilege even if they
are at the "center" in certain instances. It's possible for men to
simultaneously inhabit many worlds with different degrees of privilege
and powerlessness. Some men experience masculine privilege within a
family setting or on the job, yet they may also experience disadvantage
as, say, a black man in white-dominated settings or as a Muslim man in
white, Christian communities. Author and transman Jacob Anderson-
Minshall writes, "Becoming a man has opened my eyes to the privileges
men still have over women in this country; it's not just getting paid
more for the same work, it's a level of respect I was instantly granted

Reflections on Masculine Privilege

When I was in school, the boys took geometry and the girls took home ec. I remember thinking this was really unfair that we had to do math and the girls learned how to make a pot roast and feed a family. I thought geometry was a burden. But looking back I realize that we got an education in ways the girls didn't and there was a certain amount of privilege in that. Though in actuality, I never did use geometry in real life and it took me years to learn how to cook and wash my clothes!
—Micky Hohl, forty-four-year-old filmmaker/DJ

My ex-girlfriend is an interior designer. She used to come home and tell me about having to deal with contractors who would treat her like she's "just a girl." They'd try to get her in bed or act condescending toward her, like she didn't know what she was doing. I'm an electrician and I work with contractors, too. But they don't try to pull that shit with me.
—Donovan Davidson, thirty-eight-year-old electrician

A couple of weeks ago I was riding with a white male shuttle driver. He screamed "Bitch!" to a white woman on a bike that crossed in front of his car and surprised him as he was turning. I am a black man. Would he have screamed "Nigger!" if it had been a black woman on the bike? I don't think so. I think he was taking advantage of a privilege of perceived male sameness. I processed this. I thought about it. I had the opportunity to say something to him later but I didn't. I used a variety of excuses: My child was with me, so I waited. My partner said to let it go and I value her opinion. The driver was older and set in his ways. No sense wasting my energy on that one. This certainly was not a fireable offense.

And there lies my privilege. I can let misogyny go and not feel the direct impact of it. I've been doing antisexist work for years and I let it go. I don't have to be "on" or feel the weight of it 24/7. Sexism is still not about me; it is about "them." Until that reality changes, I have so much more work to do.

—Michael Shaw, forty-five-year-old social worker

I am a privileged, straight, white male. I don't wake up in the morning worried about where I park my car or whether I will be sexually harassed or assaulted. I don't wake up in the morning worried about being confronted because of my skin color. And I don't wake up in the morning worried about being gay bashed.

—Stephen McArthur, sixty-year-old hotline crisis worker and violence prevention educator

One thing I've noticed is that men who consider themselves feminist often take a kind of bloodless, it's-all-theory attitude toward feminist topics. I can't tell you how many conversations I've had with male friends who are feminists in which they parse arguments and make statements as if there are no actual real-world implications of what they're saying. They don't take it personally, which to me is a dead giveaway that they don't truly get the ways that sexism and gender roles damage them, too. And that's their privilege talking—because of the benefits they do get from the status quo, and also because they're taught (directly and indirectly, by both mainstream culture and by some parts of feminist culture) that sexism has to do with women only. It's a blindness and depersonalization that women and people whose genders don't fit the standard binary can't afford to have, because sexism and misogyny hit us in the face (sometimes literally) at least almost every day. But men can choose to ignore it if they want, the same way white people can avoid dealing with race by taking shelter in their white privilege.

—Lisa Jervis, thirty-six-year-old cofounder, *Bitch: Feminist Response to Pop Culture* as a white man. But it's tenuous: when others see the cane I walk with, or realize I was once a woman, in their eyes I suddenly become half a man, or not a 'real' man and some of those privileges evaporate, doors of opportunity close."

Some might assume the margin is an undesirable place to be, but hooks points out that there is a form of power in the margins. Those at the margins—the gardeners and service workers, gay men, or non-English speakers—have insight into their own worlds as well as into the world of those at the center. By contrast, those at the center *think* they know it all. They think their own worldview is everyone's worldview and they don't realize that people at the margins have a deep understanding of both worlds. The immigrant gardener knows his own neighborhood and he understands the patterns of the rich because he travels there to work. The rich don't travel to the gardener's immigrant neighborhood and, if they do, are unlikely to understand what's going on.

This understanding of two worlds doesn't offer material power (and relative disadvantage still exists in many regards), but hooks explains that it confers a certain sort of cultural currency. Living at the margins gives people insight, a window into understanding the center in ways that rarely work in reverse.

But before we "start making a checklist of who is at the top and bottom" (or at the center or the margins), Factora-Borchers has some advice: "Don't bother," she warns. "The pyramid shifts with context." The point is not to rank or to compare. The point is to learn and to make a change.

Confronting Masculine Privilege

"Pointing out that men are privileged in no way denies that bad things happen to men," writes Barry Deutsch. Privilege doesn't mean guys get an easy pass in life. Deutsch continues, "Being privileged does not mean that men do not work hard, do not suffer. In many cases—from a boy being bullied in school, to a soldier dying in war—the sexist society that maintains male privilege also does great harm to boys and men."

Some argue that men are oppressed because they aren't allowed to express a full range of emotions, they're constrained in what they can wear, and they are limited in how they are allowed to care for others. Robert Jensen argues that this is not oppression, but what he calls "toxic masculinity." "Toxic masculinity hurts men," he writes, but "there's a big difference between women dealing with the constant threat of being raped, beaten, and killed by the men in their lives, and men not being able to cry."

Yet some men have organized around the idea of their own oppression. Men's rights and fathers' rights groups argue that they face discrimination in divorce and custody decisions and that men are routinely and falsely accused of harassment or abuse. By avoiding real information about sexism, unearned privilege, and the institutionalized imbalance of power and authority, men's rights movements mask masculine privilege. There are legitimate social issues that need to be hashed out. However, the data tell us that, in the aggregate, men are not the primary victims of sexism. Masculinities expert Michael Flood clarifies that men who experience abuse, fathers who want greater involvement as parents, or male partners going through separation or divorce certainly deserve services and support. But the dangerous accusations against women by men's and fathers' rights movements create a backlash that, according to Flood, exacerbates "systematic silencing and blaming of the [actual victims] of violence" and hampers progress toward gender equality or even pushes it backward.

Many guys might reasonably say, "But I'm not like that. I'm not sexist. I don't exert masculine privilege. I'm just a regular guy." And there are plenty of great guys out there. Yet because of the institutional components of masculine privilege, it becomes difficult to simply opt out. Of course it's true that plenty of men and boys don't routinely exhibit sexist behavior and don't fling about masculine advantage like monkeys in a tree. But distancing oneself from gender politics without

Giving Up Unearned Privilege

Masculine privilege is social advantage that is derived from the happenstance of one's birth or conferred by society on certain groups. It's one thing to talk about privilege, but what would it take to give it up? Why would we want to and what might be some of the risks? Consider the following questions about giving up unearned privilege:

1. If I speak out and take action about unearned privilege, will my friends or family make fun of me or cut me out of the scene?
2. If it's a privilege not to have to think about my privilege, except when I feel like it, then what would it be like to think about masculine privilege critically and more often? And is thinking about privilege enough?
3. If I give up some of my privilege, will I put myself at a disadvantage in this competitive world?
4. Is it enough that I don't beat, cheat, or lie? If I want to refuse to be a bystander to sexism and all forms of social privilege, what do I need to do?
5. If I start taking masculine privilege seriously, won't this make me bitter? Or too serious? What if people don't want to be around me anymore? Will I feel like a traitor to other men?

actively engaging in the process to make things better tacitly enables the problems to continue. We all need to consider how we might take an active role in making a change. Otherwise we risk being part of the problem through passive denial or inaction.

In her book *Boys Will Be Boys: Breaking the Link Between Masculinity and Violence*, author Myriam Miedzian explains that what we know best, the stuff that "forms part of our everyday landscape, is also that which we most take for granted, and question the least. And some of the strongest jolts to our awareness, the deepest reorientations in our thought, often come from being confronted with the obvious." Miedzian also writes that there's the chance that challenging "assumptions, values, and patterns of behavior that have been taken for granted for so long can be threatening to people's sense of identity and self-worth; it can create feelings of guilt." Guilt, however, is a paralyzing, unproductive emotion. We need better ways to address social, political, moral, and ethical responsibilities when it comes to sexism and masculine privilege.

Relinquishing privilege involves, in part, each of us doing the work ourselves to examine our privilege. Peggy McIntosh has noticed that well-intentioned men may grant that women are disadvantaged yet be unwilling to admit to the ways that men are overprivileged. The interplay between sexism and masculine privilege penalizes women and, even by default, benefits men. Men may say they will work to improve "women's status," McIntosh says, but they can't or won't support the idea of lessening men's status. Denying masculine advantage, she continues, creates taboos around "the subject of advantages that men gain from women's disadvantages. These denials protect male privilege from being fully acknowledged, lessened, or ended."

What would compel men to confront and relinquish the unearned perks of gender? Why should men change? Michael Flood argues that men have an ethical obligation to eliminate that privilege. There is a simple moral imperative that men give up their unearned share of power. "The struggle to be ethically and morally consistent with our belief systems and our behaviors leads to complex questions and constant negotiations with self. The most important thing is that we have a responsibility to be introspective," Flood says.

Change doesn't have to mean becoming ultrasensitive, emo, passive, or constantly serious. Introspection, insight, awareness, and action can be serious. It can be done through humor. It can be private. It can mean talking with people or marching in the streets. It means educating ourselves. The challenge, according to Jackson Katz, is that in most cultures introspection is antithetical to constructed, hegemonic, dominant masculinity.

Unmasking male privilege makes each of us newly accountable. It means we have to be willing to face hard questions about how sexism is personal and political. It means being willing to take a stand about what each of us will do to make a difference.

Making Privilege Visible

The most effective male allies in our efforts to eradicate sexism are those men who understand that male privilege is not something you can remove like a coat. It operates at all times and in most instances serves to afford us unspoken and often unrecognized pleasures. It is the threat of losing the benefits of sexism that motivates most men to be silent in the face of men's violence and privilege and why male "bystanders" are not readily intervening on men's sexist aggression and/or gendered injustices. It is the threat to male privilege that also produces the vitriolic response of many men to feminism.

    —Chuck Derry, fifty-two-year-old founder, Gender Violence Institute

When men involve ourselves in antisexist and antiviolence efforts, this too is shaped by patriarchal privilege. Men's groups receive greater media attention and interest than similar groups of women, partly because of their novelty, but also because of the status and cultural legitimacy granted to men's voices in general. We receive praise and credit (especially from women), which is often out of proportion to our efforts, although this is understandable. And we are able to draw on men's institutional privilege to attract levels of support and funding rarely granted to women.

    Men can rightly claim to be antisexist, but it is a mistake to claim to be nonsexist. In patriarchal societies such as ours, all men learn sexist thoughts and behaviors, all of us receive patriarchal privileges whether we want to or not, and all of us are complicit to some degree in sexism. Our task is not to be nonsexist, as this is impossible, but to be antisexist. Yes, we can rid ourselves of particular sexist assumptions and stop practicing particular sexist behaviors, but in a sexist culture we can never be entirely free of sexism.

    —Michael Flood, forty-one-year-old researcher

I'm a pre-op FTM [female-to-male], second-generation Indian American, born and raised in Missouri. I'm female and I walk as male, so I'm constantly grappling with masculine privilege. The desire to be seen pressures me to collude with that system, but my girl upbringing makes such indifference impossible. Women's safety is a daily top priority for me, so I try and walk in ways that help women feel safe. I mean that literally. I walk a mile to and from the bus stop every day, and each night, I'm very intentional with how I walk—pace, space, and gaze—I attempt to eradicate danger from my steps in a way that supports women's occupation of space.

—S. Aakash Kishore, twenty-three-year-old lab assistant

I work at a rape crisis center doing advocacy, counseling, and prevention education. I benefit from masculine privilege every time I walk into a high school class to teach about rape. The young men, who because of sexism or defensiveness would tune out my female coworkers, listen because they've been taught to respect men, and only men. Masculine privilege allows the vast majority of men to sail through life oblivious to the day-in/day-out rape, abuse, and harassment that the women they love suffer at the hands of men.

—Patrick Donovan, thirty-year-old prevention services coordinator,
rape crisis center

I am constantly aware of the privileges our culture bestowed upon me at birth, and while I'm aware that I cannot reject these privileges, I can work against the system that gave them to me.

—Steve McAllister, thirty-year-old health educator

Chapter 5

Man Up: Getting Involved in Feminist Action

ONCE MEN START CRITICALLY ANALYZING masculine privilege and thinking about what it means to give it up, then what? What, exactly, can men do to take action and put theory into practice? How do guys "man up" and participate in feminist activism?

Men are traveling many different avenues in their quest to address crucial gender issues at home and around the world. Organizations and individuals are actively confronting sexism, supporting feminist causes, and demonstrating the tremendous transformative potential for improving gender relations, creating more equitable communities, and eradicating gender-based injustice. Men are working on global, national, community, and individual levels to end sexual objectification of women, improve reproductive rights, increase gender literacy, and prevent male violence.

Sometimes the prospect of tackling social justice issues can be overwhelming. Getting involved in politics at any level might feel pointless. We might wonder how we can make a difference, or it might seem as if our actions won't matter. It's not uncommon to feel swallowed up and disenfranchised by a system that's far bigger than we are.

Because sexism and oppression run so deeply throughout our society it can be especially hard to know where to start when it comes to supporting feminist issues. Some men become immobilized from worry that feminist women will be hostile or uninviting. Some people use assumptions and stereotypes about feminists as an excuse to remain uninvolved. But jumping the hurdles to confront these myths is one form of action. And despite legitimate concerns about political efficacy, men can lead ethical lives by getting involved with gender justice and by taking action that makes a difference.

In *Feminist Theory: From Margin to Center* bell hooks reminds us not to get bogged down by focusing on men's role in perpetuating sexism to the extent that an important point gets overlooked: "Men can lead life-affirming, meaningful lives without exploiting and oppressing women." Men and women "have been socialized to passively accept sexist ideology," hooks writes. While men don't need to blame themselves, we each have a responsibility for eliminating sexism. That means guys need to put the pedal to the metal and their feet on the street. Assuming responsibility means taking action.

This action might include making everyday choices about relationships, work, and politics that are informed by better understandings of masculinity and gender. It may mean increasing personal accountability by refusing to be a silent bystander to sexism. It might mean volunteering for a community organization working to prevent male violence against women. Or it could involve policy making and agenda setting on a state, national, or international scale.

Whether we choose to call ourselves feminist, pro-feminist, antisexist, or feminist allies, each of us can get involved in fighting sexism and all forms of discrimination by speaking up, getting smart, voting, and refusing to sit on the sidelines.

Global, National, and State Action

In the global arena, feminists from all over the world are concerned about many issues, including sex trafficking of women and girls; poverty, which disproportionately affects women; equal access to education; male violence and sexual assault, which continue to be sanctioned by tradition in many cultures; the impact of globalization on working conditions in developing countries; reproductive rights and family planning; and the HIV/AIDS pandemic. Organizations such as the United Nations and OXFAM International develop programs to assess global need and solutions. Increasingly, governments and nongovernmental organizations are paying attention to men's role in eradicating gender-based problems.

In 2003, for example, a group of experts met in Brazil for a UN conference about men and gender equality. Attendees from around the world agreed that any effective policy on poverty and HIV/AIDS has to clarify and promote men's and boys' engagement with these issues. According to the UN press release, the spread of HIV/AIDS is related to persistent stereotypes about manliness that encourage men to display sexual prowess by having multiple partners. Masculine aggression and lack of responsibility in sexual relationships causes behaviors that put men and their partners at risk. Conference attendees concluded that policymakers must consider these factors in creating successful programs. The UN also announced its finding that women's economic status is improved by cultural and government policy attention to men's taking on a greater share of domestic responsibility.

In the United States, the National Organization for Men Against Sexism (NOMAS) also supports public policy strategies for improving international economic conditions. The group's Globalization Task Force (GTF) demands alternatives to elite-led world politics, which it says "disproportionately harms marginalized and impoverished communities." The GTF believes that dominant masculinity contributes to destructive forms of globalization. The GTF starts from the understanding that masculinity is socially constructed. From there, the task force aims to promote positive modes of masculinities "at the individual, organizational, national, and global levels." By sponsoring workshops and presentations that explain men's role in globalization and by making educational and media material available to the public, the GTF gets the word out about how global power is *gendered* power. Understanding how masculinity affects global development leads to solutions that are "egalitarian, diverse, accountable, people-centered, and sustainable."

International development expert Frances Cleaver's anthology,

Masculinities Matter! Men, Gender and Development, explores a range of global interests and concerns: Hindu nationalism and masculinity in India, the role of masculinity in war in Uganda, gender and desire in Vietnam. Cleaver explains that it is critical to integrate "masculinity into the study of development." Equally vital is recognizing how globalization and neocolonial power reconfigure masculinity. Thus, for example, writes Cleaver, as transnational corporations wield influence over local economies in developing regions, subsistence farming is destroyed, creating forced migration patterns among *male* workers who leave their homes and move to "migrant enclaves, squatter camps, labour camps" in search of work. Revealing how globalization and development is gendered, according to the GTF, improves the ability to find policy solutions that promote equality, nonviolence, and democratic gender relations.

U.S. legislators are also addressing international issues. The practice of human trafficking, which affects an estimated six hundred thousand to eight hundred thousand children, teens, men, and women globally, has been of particular concern. According to the U.S. Department of Justice, between 14,500 and 17,500 of these victims are brought into the United States. Many modern-day slaves are forced into sweatshops, domestic servitude, restaurant work, and migrant agricultural work. Women and children risk being forced into stripping, prostitution, live sex shows, and other aspects of the sex-work industry. The Violence Against Women Act (VAWA) provides funding for shelters, and the Trafficking Victims Protection Act of 2000 provides ways for qualified noncitizen trafficking victims to apply for special visas and access to legal assistance, housing, and healthcare so they can begin rebuilding their lives. But again, issues such as global sex trafficking can be addressed much more thoroughly by looking at the gender dynamics at play. That means knowing not only who is providing sex for pay, but who's doing the pimping, and who's buying the services.

State-level legislative efforts also provide important avenues for promoting gender equality. Legislators, policy groups, and individual citizens work to improve gender-based conditions by advocating for reproductive rights, pay equity, and marriage laws that uphold the principles of civil liberty.

Child custody law is at the contentious center of one policy debate occurring at both the national and state levels. This debate is framed largely around ideological arguments about who is best suited to be the primary caregiver. Although reactionary and conservative fathers' rights groups claim the courts discriminate against men in custody decisions, in fact, fathers haven't often asked for custody. And when they have, the request has sometimes been used as a strategy to manipulate lower child support payments. In any case, by the late twentieth century, automatic preference for giving custody to mothers was pretty much abolished. Instead, the court's focus in custody decisions today is intended to serve the children's best interests.

Beginning in the 1970s, there was a shift away from automatic maternal preference, a policy that coincided with an increase in the number of women working outside the home. It was also consistent with efforts by feminists who wanted equal rights, not special preferences, and who wanted to avoid reinforcing essentialist stereotypes that women are "naturally" nurturing. Feminist men's groups such as NOMAS have supported gender-neutral custody decisions, figuring that custody should be given to the parent who has consistently been the primary caregiver. Men sometimes take on this role, and NOMAS thinks this should be recognized. Gender-neutral custody policies, the group explains, promote the possibilities for shifting gender roles in ways that ameliorate women's disproportionate domestic burden while also expanding men's parenting options and responsibilities. (NOMAS opposes national trends toward mandated joint custody because there is a lack of psychological and social research showing this practice is in children's best interest.)

There are many ways each of us can get involved in politics on global, national, and state levels. The American Association of University Women (AAUW) provides fact sheets and position papers on equity issues and policy decisions. This information gives easy access to anyone who wants to learn about the issues, find out where politicians stand on them, and weigh in politically. The popular blog feministing.com presents information on gender-relevant current affairs and public policy debates and provides links to a slew of similar sites full of topical information. Similarly, the group blog at The Man Files provides a forum for well-known feminists such as Michael Kimmel, Byron Hurt, Jackson Katz, and others to connect their expertise on "what it means to be a man" with current political events. The Man Files bridges communities of feminist men and women and provides a wealth of information for those who want to learn more and start getting involved with the political issues of the day.

Community and Campus Action

Men's groups and community networks around the world are confronting an array of feminist issues using such tactics as gender-awareness campaigns, mentoring for boys, peer education, and political advocacy. These groups have adopted a wide range of creative strategies that encourage men to think about sexism and that promote action.

Australian scholar Michael Flood points to a number of examples: A group in India used film to convince men to reflect on their relations with women. "Guerrilla theatre" performed in South African bars sparked discussion about gender, and in Cambodia pamphlets on masculinities issues were distributed to men in community markets. A Brazilian program called Program H was geared to "promote respectful identities and gender-equitable lifestyles among young men and women," writes Flood. Program H got the word out in ways that caught people's attention by drawing on mass media and youth culture and by creating "postcards, banners, and comics" that addressed the issues.

Social marketing campaigns also catch attention by using well-known male figures to help encourage boys and men to change their behavior. In Bangladesh campaigns have been aimed at preventing acid attacks on girls and women; in the United States they have targeted issues of sexual consent and nonviolence among young men. Gabe Kapler, former outfielder for the Boston Red Sox, has taken the lead in shifting social norms about masculinity and violence. Appearing on radio and television and in magazines, Kapler is outspoken about the problem of domestic violence, something he knows about intimately through his wife, Lisa, a survivor of violence by a former boyfriend. Together the couple is committed to preventing abuse and helping others heal. Kapler has lent a hand in getting antiviolence video broadcast on the message center above Fenway Park; he brought the issue to Bridgewater State College, speaking about male violence to a crowd of more than 550 sports fans and concerned students.

The baseball star and his wife also established the Gabe Kapler Foundation, which provides a Los Angeles battered women's shelter with childcare services and playground equipment, collaborates with the Men's Resource Center for Change, a clearinghouse for men's feminist activism in Amherst, Massachusetts, and works with Safe Passage, a shelter in Northampton, Massachusetts.

The U.S.-based group Men Can Stop Rape confronts dominant social norms through its innovative poster series, MY STRENGTH IS NOT FOR HURTING. This slogan encourages men to practice consent in their sexual relations and to rethink what masculine strength is all about. Activist and therapist Dani Meier was instrumental in creating a similar public awareness media initiative for the Real MEN's Project (Men Embracing Non-Violence). The project's antiviolence campaign included billboards and posters with slogans such as TEACH OUR SONS: REAL MEN DON'T HIT, and NO MEANS NO: REAL MEN DON'T RAPE. EVERY WOMAN IS SOMEBODY'S DAUGHTER. The campaign sent a powerful message about men's responsibility in preventing violence. In fact, the name of the group, "Real MEN's Project," explains Meier, one of the group's founders, was an attempt to refute stereotypes about "real men" as guys "who are macho, tough, and quick to violence."

The Renaissance Male Project, based in Toledo, Ohio, uses ideas of accountability and action in its ambitious efforts to, as the group puts it, "promote collaborative and reciprocal relationships between men, women, girls and boys." The Renaissance Male Project puts into practice the belief that even if men are socialized into limiting gender

Teach our sons.

Real MEN don't hit.

For information on ending domestic and sexual violence,

Call 517.783.2861

The Real MEN's Project

Real MEN's Project (Men Embracing Non-Violence) is a not-for-profit group of m son, Michigan, who believe it is the responsibility of *all* men--fathers, coaches, teac gy, business & community leaders--to teach the boys and young men in our familie communities to respect all women, to model nonviolence, to reject social pressure

Dani Meier/Real MEN's Project

The Real MEN's Project (Men Embracing Non-Violence) created this poster for a public awareness campaign. The poster describes the group as "men . . . who believe it is the responsibility of all men—fathers, coaches, teachers, clergy, business & community leaders—to teach the boys and young men in our families and our communities to respect all women, to model nonviolence, to reject social pressures that drive boys and men to hide behind a front of toughness, silence, and aggression, and to confront domestic and sexual violence wherever it exists."

roles, men *also* have profound abilities to change. The group teaches how masculinities are socially constructed, produced, and reproduced, rather than "essential" or "natural." It does this by sponsoring monthly discussions about masculinity, sexuality, and power that are led by scholars and community activists. The project also disseminates "The Black Male Privileges Checklist," a collection of examples intended to get people thinking about unearned masculine advantage, specifically through the lens of black identity. According to founder and executive director Jewel Woods, critically questioning men's relationship to power enables the group to effectively confront a range of issues, including bullying and sexism among boys, American men's role in sex tourism, the consequences of war on men and their families, and the role of race and gender in national elections.

Focusing more specifically on male sexual assault, the Riverview Center, which provides rape crisis services in Iowa, Illinois, and Wisconsin, works closely with men and boys in the community "to make men's violence against women a men's issue." When a local strip club opened in Dubuque, Iowa, executive director Josh Jasper offered violence-prevention training for all female club employees. But knowing that self-defense is only part of the solution, and with evidence that bouncers can't always prevent men from assaulting dancers, the Riverview Center launched a public awareness campaign holding men accountable for preventing verbal and physical assault. The center mounted billboards throughout the tristate area, with one sign right in front of the strip club boldly stating, REAL MEN KNOW OBJECTIFYING SOME WOMEN HURTS ALL WOMEN. The point was not to put the club out of business, explains Jasper. The effort was about "engaging men to become critical thinkers." Cid Standifer reports in the *Galena Gazette* that the billboard asked "men to think about how their actions perpetuate violence," to examine what manhood is, and to redefine masculinity.

Individual activist men such as masculinities expert Jackson Katz also take on large-scale community projects in strategizing for social change. A filmmaker, author, and *Huffington Post* blogger, Katz appears widely in media sources. He created *Tough Guise*, the acclaimed film about violence, media, and the crisis in masculinity, and he wrote *The Macho Paradox*, a book on the same subject. Katz speaks and conducts trainings on college campuses and in community settings across the United States and internationally. Katz is instrumental in coining the bystander concept—that is, how men can be actively involved with antisexism and violence prevention rather than remaining silent enablers.

Still others are engaged in community-based activism that brings together everyday men working on important feminist issues. The Men's Resource Center for Change is committed to creating models of positive masculinity. Other groups working for change include the White Ribbon Campaign, Men Stopping Violence, A Call to Men, and many more. Until 2008 Dads and Daughters had a successful ten-year run encouraging strong relationships between fathers and stepfathers and their daughters. Dads and Daughters' founder Joe Kelly continues highlighting the importance of men's active engagement in their children's lives through the blog and the website, thedadman.com.

Campus groups address countless issues and engage young men in progressive feminist politics. The Men's Leadership Project at the University of Virginia encourages men and boys to find their own authentic voice, to become gender aware, and to reimagine masculine strength in positive terms. Its mentorship program pairs undergraduate college men with fifth-grade boys to promote constructive gender identity development and leadership skills. Without question, says program director Christopher L. Wilcox Elliott, "the most transformative moments happen when these young men are asked to confront and challenge the dominant stories they have learned about masculinities and femininities." This conversation is most powerful when groups of men share their diverse backgrounds with candor and courage, Elliott says. Once this happens, the next step is teaching men "to work in partnership with groups of women advocating for similar issues of gender justice." These young men are taking action through personal politics and everyday choices to promote egalitarian families and relationships at work and at home, in the clubs, and on the streets.

Practical Strategies for Change

Do you want to propose a gender-equity policy for your campus, community, or workplace? Do you want to bring a speaker to your school to talk about masculinity or preventing male violence? Do you want to request funding for a film screening, workshop, or feminist teach-in? These guidelines can help you articulate a concrete plan and achieve your goal:

- What is your recommendation or request?
- What would it achieve?
- What is the rationale for your recommendation or request?
- How will your recommendation or program suggestion be implemented?
- Who is your target audience? How will you draw that audience to your event?
- Will you be inviting outside organizations or guest speakers to the campus? If so, how will you contact them and accommodate them when they arrive?
- How will you measure success?
- Can you link your plan to an existing program or institutional commitment? Does your school have a gender-equity policy in place? Then highlight how your proposal supports this policy.
- Highlight similar programs that have produced positive results.
- Highlight the positive (or at least neutral) cost-benefit outcome of your program, funding request, or policy suggestion.
- Create a timeline for preparations. What needs to happen first, second, and so on? How long will each step take?

Colleges and universities can play a key role in social change. Just as campuses were the hub for student activism in the 1960s and 1970s, college groups across the country today are engaging men in addressing feminist concerns and in finding solutions. Community activist and recent college graduate Katie Sipes points to the University of California campuses at Riverside and Davis, the University of Alabama, and California State University, Fresno, as examples of colleges with active feminist men's groups. Involving men in feminist student groups—or getting men's auxiliaries started—is a practical goal for so many more campuses, Sipes says. It isn't necessary to know everything there is to know about feminism, sexism, politics, or media to get involved. As Men Against Violence at the University of Alabama explains in its mission statement, "no prior education or experience with activism is required, and new guys are always welcome." Each individual's strengths are vital in the gender justice movement.

Everyday Acts Against Sexism

Across the country, everyday men are working in the feminist trenches through actions big and small. Many guys resist sexism and related forms of subjugation by committing to constructive self-examination about their interactions with people in their lives. Take Jay Poole.

Jay grew up in North Carolina with parents who were members of the Ku Klux Klan. He was taught that white supremacy was a way of life, and that "real" men hunt and do not cry. In Poole's words, he was expected to grow up to be a "good ol' boy." Yet by exploring his world, asking hard questions of himself and others, and being committed to making friends with people beyond the small circle of his town and church, Jay learned tools for rejecting racism, sexism, and homophobia. Today, Poole brings these broader, more inclusive worldviews to his role as a social worker living in the South and to his own life as an out gay man.

Rochester, New York–based author Hank Shaw calls everyday activists such as Jay Poole "stand-up guys." Many of these stand-up guys are directly involved with preventing domestic violence and assault. They've done an unusual thing, Shaw says. They have taken a stand in fighting a problem that's so often considered "a woman's issue." These men come to the movement for reasons that "are as different as the men themselves," explains Shaw. Often, though, it's because they knew someone who was hurt by male violence, or because they are survivors themselves.

Matt Held, for example, finished a military career before joining the United Auto Workers Local 2300. What followed Held no matter what he was doing were the memories of watching his abusive father beat his stepmom. With union buddies who keep the dorms running at Cornell University, Held and the facilities management team wrote and performed a theater piece about domestic violence. They combined education with entertainment and honest talk to get the word out about abuse. In Shaw's words, Held transformed his "real-world Ph.D. in family violence" from "pain into progress."

Sometimes taking action starts with a single epiphany, Shaw says. That's what happened when Marlon Cadogan walked into a crowded childcare center at the Queens, New York, Head Start where he worked. A young woman was crying. Her husband was routinely calling her a cow and hanging cow photos around the house. Now her kids were calling her a cow, too, and the political meaning of this private act became clear: This man was referring to his wife as inferior, subhuman property.

According to Shaw, Cadogan suddenly understood "an unsettling kinship between this woman's abusive family and his own family." He thought about getting served first at the dinner table. He remembered calling his girlfriend a "ho." And he suddenly realized "how easy it is for men to consider women unequal." This started Cadogan on a process of changing how he views women. He now works with other men to help them shift their views, too. "Men have been socialized to be the ruler," he comments. "But there's more we can be. If we get men to drop their macho stance, we can end violence and discrimination."

In all honesty, this may be easier said than done. Because we "live in a patriarchal culture that supports and reinforces male domination," writes Canadian author Jenn Ruddy, "when men attempt to perform their gender in ways that are caring, supportive, emotionally sensitive and gentle, they too risk becoming victims of patriarchy." Any feminist movement that is committed to an antioppressive agenda, Ruddy writes, should also be committed to making room for these men. Even

On Men and Feminism

Having moral and political convictions, even if your friends or family don't get it, is real strength. It's not like men have to be strong to be "real" men. But in our culture, that's pretty much still the message. So at least for now, as long as we're going with that story that men should be strong, let's think about how much strength it really takes to think for yourself and to take a stand against gender injustices that happen in big and small ways every single day.

—Matt Gribble, twenty-one-year-old student

Feminists supposedly hate men. But how can this be true if some feminists are men? I am a proud feminist man and have been ever since I've been inspired by feminist women—learned from them, been accepted by them, been confronted on my sexism by them. Feminist women of color, feminist lesbian and bi women, feminist women with disabilities—all have been my leaders in the feminist movement. I will be forever grateful and will call myself a feminist man for as long as they want me to.

—Ben Atherton-Zeman, forty-one-year-old spokesperson, NOMAS

I'm a women's studies major at my college. On orientation day, when I was registering for classes, a woman came up to me and asked me what my major was. I told her, and all she said was "There's a concept" with a raise of her eyebrows. This is pretty much the general reaction I get. I believe my role in feminism is to be an outspoken ally of equality across the board.

—Doug Haughey, twenty-five-year-old guy behind the counter

I hate it when a guy talks to a girl just so he can get some "action." One of the things that I do to contribute to feminism is to talk to my brother and friends about respect.

—Paolo Molina, twenty-one-year-old student

I think men need to learn to listen to women, hear what they have to say, learn to take their perspective, and only then make a suggestion.
—Arnie Kahn, sixty-six-year-old professor

I work for the Houston Area Women's Center in the training department. I cofounded an organization called "Men Against Violence" when I was in college at the University of North Texas. The work is very satisfying and at times very frustrating. It's meaningful and I can see positive changes working with other men on what are typically seen as "women's issues." But it's also difficult dismantling the male training I have been brought up with. At the end of the day, I love what I do, but there are days when I wish it were easier and that more men and women valued the work that feminists do.
—Luke McKibben, twenty-eight-year-old manager of training and volunteer services, Houston Area Women's Center

A feminist man? Isn't that an oxymoron?
I get that question fairly often. In fairness, few people have met a bearded guy who is into rock climbing, hiking, hunting, and drinking beer with his buddies—and also happens to be wearing a THIS IS WHAT A FEMINIST LOOKS LIKE T-shirt. When I tell people I work in the Women's Center and have been very involved in Men Against Violence work for several years, I get a similar reaction.
Why is a guy who is a feminist and also enjoys "manly" pursuits so confusing to us? How do men lose anything if they embrace feminism?
Gender equity is not a commodity. It isn't a scarce resource. The real oxymoron is patriarchal power. It has stolen men's sense of self and meaningful connection to others. It abuses and kills the women we care about. So why do we cling to patriarchy and fear the "F-word"?
—Jonathan Grove, twenty-nine-year-old program coordinator, Men Against Violence, Women's Center at Pacific Lutheran University

better, she argues, the "feminist movement should make room for any person—regardless of sex or gender—who is committed to dismantling patriarchy."

Media and Pop Culture

Some men are getting involved in feminist media literacy projects that offer tools for decoding the ways in which gender stereotypes are reinforced in everyday pop culture. Other men are using pop culture to reach and engage people in dialogue about gender issues and feminism.

Sut Jhally, executive director of the Media Education Foundation (MEF), promotes media literacy by exposing the sexism that runs rampant throughout music video, film, and advertising. Since its inception in 1991, the MEF has produced numerous videos for use in schools and other educational settings. Though it has made films on topics such as oil consumption and the pharmaceutical industry, the MEF is perhaps best known for its films that confront sexism and misogyny, including the *Dreamworlds* and *Killing Us Softly* series. The MEF film *Boys to Men?* raises questions about the pressures and expectations faced by a diverse group of young urban males; *Breaking Our Silence* focuses on community men who speak out against violence and domestic abuse.

The magazine *Bitch: Feminist Response to Pop Culture* also provides its readers with tools to analyze and understand sexism in pop culture. Through its quarterly print magazine and its website, *Bitch* takes on misogyny, racism, and homophobia in every form of media and pop culture, from film and TV to advertising and books. Brian Frank is operations manager at *Bitch*. Frank remarks that it was strange at first to be the only male-identified person in the office. But unlike many all-male work spaces, he says, *Bitch* is trying to move beyond gendered expectations both in the workplace and through its pop culture analysis. "There's no question that I've surprised more than a few people when they've walked into the office or called on the phone and found me on the other end of the line," Frank says with an activist wink.

Other organizations and projects are using pop culture itself to reach and engage men in discussions about gender and feminism. In 2007, a Different Kind of Dude Fest (DKDF) came together for a two-day punk festival in Washington, DC. The event was meant as a chance to challenge ideas of dominant masculinity, both within the punk community and in society at large. The Dude Fest was about guys dealing with, instead of blaming, each other for problems such as harassment in the pit and on the street. "As guys," the festival web statement comments, "we have a lot of limits on how we behave, what we feel, and who we connect with. What if we came together to talk honestly about these gender expectations and punk?"

To explore this question, DKDF featured a lineup of more than ten bands as well as workshops on masculinity, community, and how to be responsible feminist allies. Proceeds from the show went to support HIPS (Helping Individual Prostitutes Survive), a group that helps female, male, and transgender sex workers in DC lead healthy lives.

Hip-hop stars Sarah Jones and Michael Franti use music as a tool for antisexist (and anti-imperialist) politics. Rap artist Bishop Freeze uses socially conscious lyrics to inform and challenge men to take a serious look at violence, sexism, and manhood. Teaming up with the antiviolence organization A Call to Men, Bishop Freeze produced a CD, *Stand Up—Speak Out*, that reflects the group's public awareness goal: getting men to take a stand in ending violence and discrimination against women and girls.

Like music, festivals, and print magazines, grassroots blogs have also emerged as an effective pop culture outlet for writers, activists, and thinkers to publicize and debate men's issues and feminism. The blog *Fem-Men-Ist* invites readers to participate in "collaborative brainstorming and revolutionary heartstorming towards conscious community." The blog's author, Richard, describes himself as a "dj, producer, writer, activist, feminist, unapologetic straight ally." On *Fem-Men-Ist* he brings into play a melded analysis of race, gender, sexuality, and masculinity in hashing out political affairs and current events. *Rebeldad* and *Daddy Dialectic*, blogs devoted to fathering and stay-at-home dads, are hosted,

A Call to Men, www.acalltomen.org

Rap artist Bishop Freeze and the antiviolence group A Call to Men worked together to produce the CD Stand Up—Speak Out *to raise awareness about men's violence against women.*

respectively, by Brian Reid and Jeremy Adam Smith, men who are committed to caregiving and egalitarian relationships, and who see these roles for men and fathers as "more in tune with the landscape of 21st century America."

Today's media, which are both more centralized (through corporate mergers) and less (through the Internet), offer unique opportunities for activists to connect on the issues they care about. Corporate media and entertainment are all about making a buck, which often is generated through sexism and misogyny, but blogs and websites provide ways for individuals and groups to both critique corporate media and create their own forms of media and entertainment.

Preventing Male Violence and Sexual Assault

The United States faces a pressing need to dispel myths about violence, help men rethink the concepts of masculine strength and power, and educate men about refusing to be passive bystanders to other men's violence. Many men are engaged in this work to prevent male violence and sexual assault. As Hank Shaw notes, the actions these men take follow no common path: "They teach. They organize. They work with survivors. They open doors."

The Gay Men's Domestic Violence Project (GMDVP), for example, provides community education and direct services for the one in four gay, bisexual, and transgendered men who will survive intimate partner assault. Founded in 1994, the grassroots organization was founded by a gay man who survived domestic violence and an attempted murder, yet who was denied services by mainstream shelters because of his gender and sexual orientation. Misunderstandings about domestic violence and the gay community can result in deadly isolation for victims of partner abuse. The education, outreach, and support offered by GMDVP are particularly important because gay men in violent relationships can face the compounding problems of internalized homophobia and the risk of homophobia among first responders and community service providers (police, paramedics, counselors).

A Call to Men, a national organization committed to ending violence against women, understands that men have a vital role in interrupting the cycle of violence. Cofounders Tony Porter, Brenda Ross, and Ted Bunch challenge men to accept "responsibility that violence against women will not end until men become part of the solution to end it." They insist on ending excuses for men's behavior that pathologize "men's violence by blaming mental illness, lack of anger management, chemical dependency, stress, etc." Such justifications only excuse men's violent behavior, the trio writes. "Violence against women is rooted in the historic oppression of women—sexism." To change these conditions means accepting leadership from women, speaking up, and refusing to support any institution or resources that are used to justify men's violence. Remaining silent is not an option because it results in passively colluding in sexism, racism, homophobia, or classism. Instead, A Call to Men provides concrete suggestions for what men can do to prevent violence against women, such as acknowledging and understanding how "sexism, male dominance and male privilege lay the foundation for all forms of violence against women," not colluding in sexism with other men, and remembering "that our silence is affirming. When we choose not to speak out against men's violence," Bunch and Porter explain in *Voice Male*, "we are supporting it."

One in Four is a national nonprofit organization specifically dedicated to rape prevention. The group's name is drawn from data that

What Men Can Do to Prevent Gender Violence

1. Approach gender violence as a *men's* issue involving men of all ages and socioeconomic, racial, and ethnic backgrounds. . . .
2. If a brother, friend, classmate, or teammate is abusing his female partner—or is disrespectful or abusive to girls and women in general—don't look the other way. . . . DON'T REMAIN SILENT.
3. Have the courage to look inward. Question your own attitudes. Don't be defensive. . . . Try hard to understand how your own attitudes and actions might inadvertently perpetuate sexism and violence, and work toward changing them.
4. If you suspect that a woman close to you is being abused or has been sexually assaulted, . . . ask if you can help.
5. If you are emotionally, psychologically, physically, or sexually abusive to women, or have been in the past, seek professional help NOW.
6. Be an ally to women who are working to end all forms of gender violence. Support the work of campus-based women's centers. . . . Raise money for community-based rape crisis centers and battered women's shelters. If you belong to a team or fraternity, or another student group, organize a fund-raiser.
7. Recognize and speak out against homophobia and gay-bashing.

indicate one in four college women have survived rape or attempted rape. Aiming to educate young men nationwide, One in Four hosts all-male programs at high schools, on college campuses, and in the military. Its strategy is based on evidence that teaching guys to be supportive allies to women and survivors reduces men's likelihood of raping. "Statistics can change," the One in Four website states. "And men can help."

Grantlin Schafer, who participated in One in Four's cross-country RV tour after graduating from college, recounts the experience in his essay "Breaking the Silence One Mile at a Time." He writes that the group met with "Plenty of stares, some thumbs up, a middle finger, countless inappropriate jokes, and the miracle question: Why are you doing this?" The reason for Schafer is simple yet profound. It's about

Discrimination and violence against lesbians and gays are wrong. This abuse also has direct links to sexism (e.g., the sexual orientation of men who speak out against sexism is often questioned, a conscious or unconscious strategy intended to silence them. This is a key reason few men do so.).

8. Attend programs, take courses, watch films, and read articles and books about multicultural masculinities, gender inequality, and the root causes of gender violence. Educate yourself and others about how larger social forces affect the conflicts between individual men and women.

9. Don't fund sexism. Refuse to purchase any magazine, rent any video, subscribe to any website, or buy any music that portrays girls or women in a sexually degrading or abusive manner. Protest sexism in the media.

10. Mentor and teach young boys about how to be men in ways that don't involve degrading or abusing girls and women. Volunteer to work with gender violence–prevention programs, including anti-sexist men's programs. Lead by example.

From Jackson Katz's "10 Things Men Can Do to Prevent Gender Violence," www.jacksonkatz.com.

taking action, he explains. "We were speaking out. We were breaking the silence: Men were finally talking about men's violence against women." And they did it without grandstanding, lecturing to people, or looking down at the audience. "We crafted our message to speak to our peers as guys who did not want to hurt women." Instead, they talked about things that guys can do to make a difference, such as not joking about rape, not minimizing the crime by using words out of context. Schafer explains that refusing to say things such as "That team just got raped," or "Get up, don't be such a pussy," or "You threw that pass like a girl" are everyday actions any of us can take to prevent a culture of violence against women. Guys who use this language probably aren't intending to hurt women, Schafer explains, but "this language equates women with being less valuable than men. Some men will use this language to justify treating women as though they are weak and inferior." *Not* using this language, and refusing to be silently complicit when others do, can really make a difference.

The need to prevent male violence is urgent because of its tremendous personal impact. A man batters a woman every eighteen seconds in this country. Male violence against women costs employers $35 billion annually. In Los Angeles, the 2008 Policy Summit on Ending Violence Against Women reports that seven thousand workers are killed each year in the workplace. The largest single category of murdered women die from domestic violence. Employers lose 9.5 million days of activity because of domestic violence. One fifth of workdays women miss are due to male violence and domestic abuse.

Domestic violence, sexual abuse, and homicide by intimate partners cost the U.S. healthcare system $5.8 billion a year. Families experiencing domestic violence visit the emergency room six times more often than other families. Domestic violence costs are greater than the costs of cancer in women and motor vehicle accidents.

Shelter programs for abused women and their children are working well, but there's a need for more of them. Additionally, there's a need for effective support programs for men and boys who are survivors of male violence and sexual assault.

Gender Justice at Home

Author Ian Law writes in his essay "Adopting the Principle of Pro-Feminism" that being pro-feminist means confronting habits that perpetuate male dominance in relationships and daily life. Law realized he could walk his talk by refusing to dominate airspace and by not insisting his views got heard all the time. It's important that men listen and understand others, he writes, instead of feeling as if guys have to solve problems, come up with solutions, and keep control of decision making. Law explains that *cooperating* doesn't mean losing control.

Men can also support feminist change by taking on more of what has been traditionally considered "women's work" in the home. Decades of feminist work has convinced us that women can do what men can do. The challenge now, writes feminist activist Gloria Steinem, is "to convince the majority of the country—and ourselves—that men can do what women can do." Otherwise, "the double burden of working inside and outside the home—always a reality for poor women, and now one for middle-class women, too—will continue to be the problem most shared by American women nationwide. Let's face it," Steinem says, "until men are fully equal inside the home, women will never be really equal outside it."

One way to take action is by bringing our politics home. Literally. It's important to take a fresh look at the gendered division of household labor, Nighat Gandhi writes in "Can Men Be the Allies of Feminism?" This is an avenue for politically significant change that's within anyone's reach. "Housework is work that is unacknowledged as work," Gandhi writes, "since most of it is unpaid work done by women." Active solidarity involves feminist or antisexist men participating completely in housework—doing dishes, changing diapers, mopping floors. (And, yes, equality also includes women taking out the trash and fixing busted pipes.) Passive sympathizing for an overworked female partner, "helping" around the house, "babysitting" one's own children, or sharing the work only after someone else asks is not the same thing as showing initiative, rolling up the shirtsleeves, and taking care of business.

Gradually, more men are choosing to do this domestic work by becoming stay-at-home dads and primary caregivers for their kids. (And many more who can't be full-time dads because of financial constraints find other ways to split the domestic load with their female partners.) Jeremy Adam Smith, author of *The Daddy Shift: How Stay-at-Home Fathers, Breadwinning Mothers, and Shared Parenting Are Transforming the Twenty-First-Century Family*, was a longtime stay-at-home dad himself. Smith sees the daddy shift as a transition away from defining fatherhood as pure breadwinning to one that encompasses capacities for both breadwinning and caregiving. Smith cautions that the number of full-time dads is still small and the accolades they receive are usually disproportionate to their numbers or their efforts. But stay-at-home dads are signs of significant hope. Smith writes that they are "bellwethers of a wider change in the culture, toward more flexible definitions of masculinity and femininity. Thanks to feminism . . . women now have more choices. So do men." Families are evolving, and so are men and ideas about masculinity.

Refusing to Be a Bystander

Most men are *good* men. *All* men are products of our culture. Many men do not behave in sexist ways. Most men do not rape, molest, or hit. The majority of men do not sexually harass women at work. And yet most men aren't doing transformative or preventive work either. If we don't take intentional action, we're letting sexism happen. We're bystanders to the problem.

Because the links between masculinity, violence, and sexism result from years of socialization, tools for unlearning and relearning behaviors and expectations are so important. According to Jackson Katz, it's time we raise the bar. Just saying, "I'm not sexist," or "I don't beat my girlfriend," is not enough. We need more men to challenge other men's sexism as it manifests in all sorts of ways. Men must refuse to be bystanders. What this requires, writes author-activist Rob Okun in his editorial "A Call to Men: From Bystanders to Activists," is men rejecting the culture of violence and shifting "their role from men-as-bystanders to men-taking-action."

To bluntly explain the bystander problem, here are a few examples: Violence on the street or women's screams for help from inside their homes often go ignored. We turn the other way and pretend not to notice. Our culture of isolated individualism trains us to ignore or fear strangers in need. Even if it's understandable that folks might not want to put themselves in the middle of a violent situation, what about letting sexist jokes go unchallenged or staying silent when guys catcall women from their cars? These are examples of the bystander problem, too.

Although taking action might push us out of our comfort zone, there are lots of ways to step up (without risking our personal safety). We might say something when family, friends, or coworkers objectify women or call people "fags." If we see a woman getting hurt, we might ask if she needs help or call the police. Men can get involved in a campus or community men's antiviolence group. Or if there isn't one, there's a great opportunity to start one.

As Dani Meier of the Real MEN's Project explains, "We believe real men are good, strong, loving, and capable of rejecting violence." The RMP's goals are about "stopping violence before it happens through education, [and] public awareness . . . as well as through reaching out to adult men who might be silent bystanders to violence around them." We want those bystanders, says Meier, "to speak up and to challenge that violence."

If we see someone getting hurt or harassed and we choose to do nothing, we're actually complicit through our silence. Yet our culture doesn't offer much support for those who want to take a stand against sexism, prejudice, and abuse. We're often encouraged to think it's okay to look the other way. For instance, research on university campuses reveals that a lot of men privately disagree with sexism and misogyny, but far fewer are willing to come forward in public with their feminist, egalitarian opinions. This results in a secondary problem: Men *think* other guys are a lot more sexist than they really are because nobody's actually talking out loud about how they really feel. The simple term, as clichéd as it might sound, is "peer pressure." Few men want to be the social outsider, so the problem perpetuates itself.

Shifting social norms and confronting the bystander phenomenon means encouraging men (and women) "to undermine men's conformity to sexist peer norms and increase their willingness to intervene in violent behavior," says Michael Flood in "Involving Men in Efforts to End Violence Against Women." Flood writes that by gathering and publicizing data on what men really think, and by using a bystander intervention model, campus and community campaigns encourage "a sense of responsibility and empowerment for ending sexual violence on the shoulders of all community members. They teach men skills to de-escalate risky situations and be effective allies for survivors, and they foster a sense of community responsibility for violence prevention."

On Bystanders

Ending violence against women is primarily the responsibility of men. Although historically it has been almost entirely women who have been at the forefront addressing this issue, we think it is essential that men play a primary role in the solution to end it. To do that, well-meaning men—men who, for the most part, don't see themselves as part of the problem—need to get involved. We are empowered bystanders. We give permission for abuse and violence when we remain silent.

—Tony Porter and Ted Bunch, fifty- and forty-seven-year-old
cofounders, A Call to Men

My cousin and I were parked on the side of the road right next to a McDonald's enjoying our dinner. We noticed that across the street a girl was arguing with someone who seemed to be her boyfriend. My cousin Sergio and I didn't think much about it after all; couples do fight. So we kept eating until we heard the girl scream, "Stop!" Then we saw what was going on. This guy was holding her by her arm and dragging her against her will. She kept yelling and my cousin and I hopped out of my car and yelled at the guy to let her go. She was crying and bawling by this point. Her "man" yelled for us to f@#k off. My cousin, being a hothead, started to cross the street and so I followed.

The boyfriend felt threatened by us and let the girl go. The guy got into his car and drove off yelling at us like a coward. The girl was so

The One in Four program, first established by MVP, follows this model by urging guys "to step up and say something when they hear bragging about getting a girl wasted at a party the night before, taking advantage of her, and other tales of conquest," writes Grantlin Schafer. He explains that it's likely "that other guys hearing this kind of talk in the dining hall or in the locker room aren't into it and are feeling uncomfortable. They're just not saying anything about it. By your standing up and speaking out, other guys will respect you, Schafer says. And "even if some guys act like they don't respect you, remember that you were the one who had the courage to do the right thing."

frightened by that point that she didn't trust us. I didn't blame her. We asked her where she lived and she said she lived only a few blocks away so we offered her a ride home. She nervously said no, but my cousin offered her his phone so she could call for a ride. She called her sister and about five minutes later she was gone.

Props to guys who speak up if their friends are being assholes and hitting on women, or whatever, instead of being silent bystanders.

—Jorge Hernandez, twenty-three-year-old credit union employee

I volunteer at our local YWCA Crisis Center, and I am amazed that I am one of only two male volunteers for this amazing organization. This shelter helps our daughters, sisters, mothers, and our friends. Why aren't men taking more of a stand to protect and help the people we love most? I believe that men are the missing key in the movement to eliminate domestic violence. In order to break the cycle of violence, men must be outspoken and become role models for boys in the way they should treat others.

—Luke Anton, twenty-five-year-old activist

I realized about two years ago that I couldn't call myself a feminist if I wasn't doing any feminist work. Pretending to be an ally in word alone was not enough. I started volunteering at my local rape crisis center after that moment.

—Dave Rini, twenty-five-year-old volunteer, rape crisis center

There are plenty of ways we can educate ourselves and take intentional action to begin shifting sexist social norms. Katz suggests that we can "attend programs, take courses, watch films, and read articles and books about multicultural masculinities." We can start learning about gender inequality and the root causes of gender violence. We can educate ourselves about how institutional and individual forces affect the conflicts between some men and women.

Getting down to the nitty-gritty means speaking up to our friends when they catcall girls on the street. It means declining to fund sexism by choosing not to buy magazines, videos, music, or online sources that are sexually degrading. Refusing to be a bystander means speaking up, sending emails, blogging, and sharing our opinions when we see sexism in the media, on the streets, or in our homes.

Taking action means being willing to stop saying, "I'm not a feminist, but. . . ." It means dissolving stereotypes that all feminists are women, that all feminist women are manhaters, and that feminist men are an oxymoron. Correcting media images that misrepresent feminists as monolithic is also important, writes Jenn Ruddy in "Gender Mending: Men, Masculinity, and Feminism," because feminism is actually a movement of diverse people with often-conflicting ideas. When men get involved in fighting sexism, it's a first step toward expanding feminism's image.

What Still Needs to Be Done

Feminist men have had a lot of success in challenging sexism. But there's a lot more that needs to be done. As the Supreme Court whittles away at *Roe v. Wade*, the landmark decision that protects a woman's right to choose abortion, the battle over reproductive rights is raging in many state legislatures. Regardless of what people choose in their personal lives, political liberties are at stake and men's participation in protecting this autonomy is so important. Other urgent areas of concern include providing services and support for veterans who are returning home affected by war trauma, for incarcerated men affected by histories of violence, and for youth who grow up with abuse. This list might seem daunting, but change is possible.

To achieve a shift in social norms surrounding masculinity, gender, and power, staff members at our jobs, administrators at our schools, and people in positions of power, authority, and leadership—especially men—must be trained to understand how to identify sexual objectification and sexism. Katz suggests that men in leadership positions can be incredibly effective in promoting change because of their ability to set agendas and establish institutional priorities that put gender equity at the top of the list. If the athletics director at a high school or college requires educational programs about masculinity and male violence, says Katz, the soccer team, the basketball team, the football team, and the lacrosse team will sit up, take notice, and participate.

Boys in high school can volunteer at domestic violence agencies. College men can work to end sexism by participating in campus Clothesline Projects and Take Back the Night marches. Men can work in childcare centers, get masculinities and gender courses into the curriculum at universities, and work to get funding for and institutionalize gender education programs. We can all strategize and build coalitions across gender, age, and political perspective.

Pop culture media can be put to good use in all sorts of ways. A working group at the 2008 Los Angeles Policy Summit on Ending Violence Against Women recommended that Hollywood create public service announcements challenging television viewers to think about masculinity more critically. TV, film, YouTube, websites, and blogs can be used to promote conversations about men's accountability in reproductive choices, fatherhood, pay equity, gay and lesbian rights, and race relations. The entertainment industry can ask tough questions of itself about how it portrays masculinity in ways that perpetuate violence.

To make sure we see lasting, long-term positive change, it's crucial that men are invested in creating institutional structures that promote this change. One effective avenue is to implement gender literacy programs in school so that kids are taught from the time they're young that knowing how to "decode" assumptions and stereotypes about gender is an important component of civic engagement.

Education about violence, bullying, and covert sexism must be integrated into mainstream curricula to emphasize that sexism, racism, and homophobia are core, not peripheral, issues. Information about gender politics must be melded into extracurricular activities, in the arts, and in athletics. These conversations don't have to be boring! Gender literacy means, for example, talking openly and honestly about sexual pleasure and sexual consent, exploring ways to understand pop culture media, learning to identify what matters to us and why, and figuring out innovative ways to take action when staying silent no longer seems a viable option. Gender literacy isn't about legislating morality; it's about encouraging broader options and better critical-thinking skills.

Shout Out to All the Stand-Up Guys and Grrrls

Men can do a tremendous amount of work to stop gender-based problems *before* they ever happen. Prevention is the real solution. And even if it seems daunting sometimes, change really is possible. Remember the Cherry Bust story from Chapter 1? Organizers and concerned campus activists at one university successfully convinced fraternity leaders and the university president that party slogans such as "We won't pull out until the cherry pops" are demeaning and dangerous to women. Letter-writing campaigns to highly ranked administrators, media coverage, and relentless educational efforts proved successful. While certainly not all the partygoers understand (or care about) the connection between language and gender politics, getting the name of the party changed and removing misogynist slogans from T-shirts and flyers were a start. It also provided the fraternities and their leadership the opportunity to rethink their community roles and their public accountability.

A lot of work is to be done and there are so many people committed to progressive change—men and women, working guys and students, trannies and genderqueers out there transforming masculinity, preventing male violence and sexual assault, increasing gender equity, and promoting change wherever necessary. Props to all the stand-up guys and grrrls who put themselves on the line and are willing to speak up and take a stand.

In the summer of 2008 some of these stand-up guys—religious leaders, executives, politicians, and activists in Hawaii—were spurred to action when men's domestic violence took the lives of nine women in the first seven months of the year. Mohamed Elmallah told newspaper reporter Rob Perez, "As an individual and a Muslim and a man," he believes domestic violence is "something we have to stop." Richard

Rodrigues Jr. joined the demonstration because of four generations of abuse in his extended family.

A large sign held up high at the protest stated, VIOLENCE CAN'T BE ENDED IN A DAY, BUT WOULDN'T TODAY BE A GOOD DAY TO START?

To borrow this thought from the good gentlemen of Hawaii: Sexism, misogyny, subjugation, and the abuse and misuse of power can't be ended in a day. But today would be a very good day to start.

READER'S GUIDE

Questions for Discussion

Do you consider yourself a feminist? What does that mean to you?

What do you think when people tell you they identify as feminists? Does your reaction differ depending on the person's sex or gender?

Do you think some men are feminist in theory but not in practice? What does this mean, and why do you think it might happen?

How early do you think little boys are taught how to be masculine? How are they taught this? Can you remember ways that you were taught what it meant to "be a man"?

Why does our culture sometimes associate masculinity with lesbians and femininity with gay men? Do you think people confuse gender status with sexual orientation?

How has gender privilege affected your daily life? What are some specific examples?

Do you think that male feminists are treated differently from female feminists? Do male feminists receive more positive attention than female feminists? Are their ideas disregarded or dismissed? What sorts of issues do these questions raise?

How does (or might) men's involvement in feminism change it?

What does it mean to be a feminist ally? What sorts of things do guys have to do to be an ally?

What is the difference between feeling guilty and taking action? What challenges does male guilt present for taking action?

Based on your experience, does race, sexual orientation, ethnicity, religion, or class status influence how you define masculinity? What are some examples?

Who are some examples of public or famous pro-feminist men?

What do you think needs to change in order for more men to fight for gender equity?

Topics for Research

Male Feminist Organizations

Questions to consider: Are there any male feminist organizations in your city or state? If yes, what impact have they made in your community? What are the main issues they are working on? If there are no male feminist organizations in your area, why do you think this is the case?

Race, Ethnicity, Class, Religion, and Masculinity

Look at magazines, websites, and other media targeted at men of different races, ethnicities, classes, and religions. What do you notice about how men are portrayed in these publications? Do ideas and expectations related to masculinity differ for men depending on race, class, and ethnicity? If so, how? How does religion seem to influence expectations about masculinity? What are the social consequences for those men who do not meet these expectations?

Issues and Activism

Pick one feminist issue—for instance, reproductive rights, pay equity, domestic violence, sexual assault and rape—and research men's historical or contemporary contribution to feminist progress. What arguments and actions did/do men use to support the cause?

Ideas for Action

Get involved in feminist groups or start one!

Write about gender justice. Start a blog, publish a zine, send an e-blast, or post something on Facebook about the gender issues that matter to you.

Go to a Take Back the Night march or vigil.

If you're in college, enroll in a women's studies or gender studies course.

Volunteer at a local rape crisis shelter or domestic violence resource center. Initiate a clothing drive for your local shelter or crisis center.

If you're a musician or artist, organize a benefit show to raise awareness or money for feminist causes.

Speak up when you hear sexist jokes or comments.

Whenever possible, buy items that are fair trade. Your dollars will show that you support fair work policies, pay, and treatment for women and men.

Try to engage your friends and family members in conversations about the privileges involved in race, class, gender, sexuality, and so on.

Write to your government officials urging them to support policies that promote sex and gender rights. Send letters and emails to radio talk shows, magazines, and other media about sexist or racist content. Speak out. Speak your truth!

Vote! Support the candidates who are serious about improving the lives of women and all people.

FURTHER READING AND RESOURCES

BOOKS

Akbar, Naim. *Visions for Black Men*. Nashville, TN: Mind Productions and Associations, 1992.

Allister, Mark. *Eco-Man: New Perspectives on Masculinity and Nature (Under the Sign of Nature)*. Charlottesville: University of Virginia, 2004.

Anderson, Eric. *In The Game: Gay Athletes and the Cult of Masculinity*. Albany: State University of New York, 2005.

Basso, Matthew. *Across the Great Divide: Cultures of Manhood in the American West*. New York: Routledge, 2001.

Beynon, John. *Masculinities and Culture*. Buckingam, UK: Open University, 2002.

Bly, Robert. *Iron John: A Book About Men*. Cambridge, MA: Da Capo, 2004.

Boone, Joseph A., and Michael Cadden. *Engendering Men: The Question of Male Feminist Criticism*. New York: Routledge, 1990.

Bordo, Susan. *The Male Body: A New Look at Men in Public and in Private*. New York: Farrar, Straus and Giroux, 2000.

Brownmiller, Susan. *Against Our Will: Men, Women and Rape*. New York: Simon & Schuster, 1975.

Butler, Judith. *Gender Trouble: Feminism and the Subversion of Identity*. New York: Routledge, 1990.

Byrd, Rudolph P., and Beverly Guy-Sheftall, eds. *Traps: African American Men on Gender and Sexuality*. Bloomington: Indiana University, 2003.

Campbell, Hugh, Michael Mayerfield Bell, and Margaret Finney, eds. *Country Boys: Masculinity and Rural Life*. University Park: Pennsylvania State University, 2006.

Chauncey, George. *Gay New York: Gender, Urban Culture, and the Making of the Gay Male World, 1890–1940*. New York: Basic, 1995.

Clatterbaugh, Ken. *Contemporary Perspectives on Masculinity: Men, Women, and Politics in Modern Society*. 2nd ed. Boulder, CO: Westview, 1996.

Coltrane, Scott. *Family Man: Fatherhood, Housework, and Gender Equity*. New York: Oxford University, 1997.

Connell, R. W. *Masculinities*. 2nd ed. Berkeley: University of California, 2005.

————. *The Men and the Boys.* Berkeley: University of California, 2001.

Digby, Tom, ed. *Men Doing Feminism (Thinking Gender).* New York: Routledge, 1998.

Eng, David. *Racial Castration: Managing Masculinity in Asian America.* Durham, NC: Duke University, 2001.

Espiritu, Yen Le. *Asian American Women and Men: Labor, Laws, and Love (The Gender Lens).* Lanham, MD: Rowman & Littlefield, 2008.

Faludi, Susan. *Stiffed: The Betrayal of the American Man.* New York: HarperCollins, 2000.

Gardiner, Judith Kegan, ed. *Masculinity Studies and Feminist Theory.* New York: Columbia University, 2002.

Ghoussoub, Mai, and Emma Sinclair-Webb, eds. *Imagined Masculinities: Male Identity and Culture in the Modern Middle East.* London: Saqi, 2000.

Gilmore, David D. *Manhood in the Making: Cultural Concepts of Masculinity.* New Haven, CT: Yale University, 1990.

González, Ray, ed. *Muy Macho: Latino Men Confront Their Manhood.* New York: Anchor, 1996.

Gutmann, Matthew C., ed. *Changing Men and Masculinities in Latin America.* Durham, NC: Duke University, 2003.

Halberstam, Judith. *Female Masculinity.* Durham, NC: Duke University, 1998.

Harper, Hill. *Letters to a Young Brother: MANifest Your Destiny.* New York: Gotham, 2007.

hooks, bell. *Feminist Theory: From Margin to Center.* Cambridge, MA: South End, 2000.

————. *We Real Cool: Black Men and Masculinity.* New York: Routledge, 2004.

Hopkinson, Natalie, and Natalie Y. Moore. *Deconstructing Tyrone: A New Look at Black Masculinity in the Hip-Hop Generation.* San Francisco: Cleis, 2006.

Hoppe, Trevor, ed. *Beyond Masculinity: Essays by Queer Men on Gender and Politics.* www.beyondmasculinity.com.

Jackson, Peter, Nick Stevenson, and Kate Brooks. *Making Sense of Men's Magazines.* Cambridge, UK: Polity, 2001.

Jarman-Ivens, Freya, ed. *Oh Boy! Masculinities and Popular Music.* New York: Routledge, 2007.

Jensen, Robert. *Getting Off: Pornography and the End of Masculinity.* Cambridge, MA: South End, 2007.

Johnson, Allan G. *The Gender Knot: Unraveling Our Patriarchal Legacy.* Philadelphia: Temple University, 1997.

Katz, Jackson. *The Macho Paradox: Why Some Men Hurt Women and How All Men Can Help.* Naperville, IL: Sourcebooks, 2006.

Kimmel, Michael S. *Manhood in America: A Cultural History.* New York: Oxford University, 1995.

————. *The Gender of Desire: Essays on Male Sexuality.* Albany: State University of New York, 2005.

———. *The Gendered Society.* New York: Oxford University, 2007.

———. *Guyland: The Perilous World Where Boys Become Men.* New York: HarperCollins, 2008.

———. *The History of Men: Essays on the History of American and British Masculinities.* Albany: State University of New York, 2005.

Kimmel, Michael S., and Michael A. Messner eds. *Men's Lives.* 7th ed. San Francisco: Pearson, 2007.

Kimmel, Michael S., and Thomas E. Mosmiller, eds. *Against the Tide: Pro-Feminist Men in the United States, 1776–1990: A Documentary History.* Boston: Beacon, 1992.

Kivel, Paul. *Men's Work: How to Stop the Violence That Tears Our Lives Apart.* Center City, MN: Hazelden, 1998.

Lamont, Michèle. *The Dignity of Working Men: Morality and Boundaries of Race, Class, and Immigration.* Cambridge, MA: Harvard University, 2000.

Lopes, Anne, and Gary Roth. *Men's Feminism: August Bebel and the German Socialist Movement.* Amherst, NY: Humanity, 2000.

Madhubuti, Haki R. *Black Men: Obsolete, Single, Dangerous? The Afrikan American Family in Transition.* Chicago: Third World, 1991.

Magnuson, Eric. *Changing Men, Transforming Culture: Inside the Men's Movement.* Boulder, CO: Paradigm, 2007.

Majors, Richard, and Janet Mancini Billson. *Cool Pose: Dilemmas of Black Manhood in America.* New York: Simon & Schuster, 1993.

Martin, Fran, Peter A. Jackson, Mark McLelland, and Audrey Yue, eds. *AsiaPacifiQueer: Rethinking Genders and Sexualities.* Urbana: University of Illinois, 2008.

Mattilda (a.k.a. Matt Bernstein Sycamore), ed. *Nobody Passes: Rejecting the Rules of Gender and Conformity.* Emeryville, CA: Seal, 2006.

Messner, Michael A. *Politics of Masculinities: Men in Movements (The Gender Lens).* Thousand Oaks, CA: Sage, 1997.

Mirandé, Alfredo. *Hombres y Machos: Masculinity and Latino Culture.* Boulder, CO: Westview, 1997.

Nanda, Serena. *Gender Diversity: Crosscultural Variations.* Prospect Heights, IL: Waveland, 1999.

Neal, Mark Anthony. *New Black Man.* New York: Routledge, 2006.

Nestle, Joan, Clare Howell, and Riki Wilchins, eds. *GenderQueer: Voices from Beyond the Sexual Binary.* Los Angeles: Alyson, 2002.

Ouzgane, Lahoucine, ed. *Islamic Masculinities.* London: Zed, 2006.

Pascoe, C. J. *Dude, You're a Fag: Masculinity and Sexuality in High School.* Berkeley: University of California, 2007.

Powell, Kevin, ed. *Who's Gonna Take the Weight: Manhood, Race, and Power in America.* New York: Three Rivers, 2003.

———. *The Black Male Handbook: A Blueprint for Life.* New York: Atria, 2008.

Rotundo, E. Anthony. *American Manhood: Transformations in Masculinity from the Revolution to the Modern Era.* New York: Basic, 1994.

Salzman, Marian, Ira Matathia, and Ann O'Reilly. *The Future of Men: The Rise of the Übersexual and What He Means for Marketing Today.* New York: Palgrave Macmillan, 2005.

Schacht, Steven P., and Doris W. Ewing, eds. *Feminism and Men: Reconstructing Gender Relations.* New York: New York University, 1998.

Shaffer, Susan Morris, and Linda Perlman Gordon. *Why Boys Don't Talk—And Why It Matters: A Parent's Survival Guide to Connecting with Your Teen.* New York: McGraw-Hill, 2004.

Sharpley-Whiting, T. Denean. *Pimps Up, Ho's Down: Hip-Hop's Hold on Young Black Women.* New York: New York University, 2007.

Smith, Jeremy Adam. *The Daddy Shift: How Stay-at-Home Fathers, Breadwinning Mothers, and Shared Parenting Are Transforming the Twenty-First-Century Family.* Boston: Beacon, 2009.

Tarrant, Shira, ed. *Men Speak Out: Views on Gender, Sex, and Power.* New York: Routledge, 2008.

Tungate, Mark. *Branded Male: Marketing to Men.* Philadelphia: Kogan Page, 2008.

Whannel, Garry. *Media Sport Stars: Masculinities and Moralities.* New York: Routledge, 2002.

ARTICLES

Flood, Michael. "Frequently Asked Questions About Pro-Feminist Men and Pro-Feminist Men's Politics." 3rd ed., revised January 3, 2002. www.xyonline.net/misc/pffaq.html

Halberstam, Judith. "Dumb & Getting Dumber: Sideways, Spongebob, and the New Masculinity." *Bitch: Feminist Response to Pop Culture*, no. 28 (Spring 2005), pp. 36–39, 92. http://bitchmagazine.org/article/dumb-getting-dumber

Kivel, Paul. "Boys Will Be Men: Guiding Your Sons from Boyhood to Manhood." 2006. www.paulkivel.com/articles/boyswillbemen.pdf

———. "Jewish Male Violence." 2007. www.paulkivel.com/articles/jewishmaleviolence.pdf

———. "Men's Work—To Stop Male Violence." 2007. www.paulkivel.com/articles/tostopmaleviolence.pdf

FILMS

Barack and Curtis: Manhood, Power and Respect. Directed by Byron Hurt. God Bless the Child Productions, 2008. Funded by the National Black Programming Consortium, the Independent Television Service, and the Ford Foundation. Available on YouTube.

Blink. Directed by Elizabeth Thompson. Independent Television Service, 2000.

Boys to Men? Directed by Frederick Marx. A Warrior Educational Films Production, 2004.

Boys Will Be Men. Directed by Tom Weidlinger. Moira Productions, 2002.

Choices: The Good, the Bad, the Ugly. Directed by Tamara Jenkins. Scenarios USA, 2004.

Cut. Directed by Elizabeth Pearson and Sally Rubin. Fanlight Productions, 2003.

Dreamworlds 3: Desire, Sex, and Power in Music Video. Directed by Sut Jhally. Media Education Foundation, 2007.

Fatherhood USA, Part I: Dedicated, Not Deadbeat. Directed by Marion Lipschutz and Rose Rosenblatt. Incite Pictures, 1998.

Fatherhood USA, Part II: Juggling Family and Work. Directed by Marion Lipschutz and Rose Rosenblatt. Incite Pictures, 1998.

A Gathering of Men. Directed by Robert Bly. Public Affairs Television, 1990.

Hip-Hop: Beyond Beats and Rhymes. Directed by Byron Hurt. God Bless the Child Productions, 2006.

I Am a Man: Black Masculinity in America. Directed by Byron Hurt. God Bless the Child Productions, 1998.

Men Talk Sex. Directed by Donald Bull and James Mulryan. Fanlight Productions, 1996.

Michael Kimmel on Gender: Mars, Venus or Planet Earth? Women and Men in a New Millennium. Media Education Foundation, 2008.

The Monster. Directed by Adam Davidson. Scenarios USA, 2000.

NO! The Rape Documentary. Directed by Aishah Shahidah Simmons. AfroLez Productions, 2006.

Prejudice: More Than Black and White. Films for the Humanities and Sciences/Films Media Group, 2008.

The Smell of Burning Ants. Directed by Jay Rosenblatt. Jay Rosenblatt Films, 1994.

Spin the Bottle: Sex, Lies and Alcohol. With Jean Kilbourne and Jackson Katz. Media Education Foundation, 2004.

Tal Como Somos: *The Latino GBT Community.* Films Media Group, 2007.

Tough Guise: Violence, Media and the Crisis in Masculinity. Featuring Jackson Katz, directed by Sut Jhally. Media Education Foundation, 1999.

Wrestling with Manhood: Boys, Bullying and Battering. Directed by Sut Jhally. Media Education Foundation, 2002.

You Don't Know Dick: Courageous Hearts of Transsexual Men. Directed by Bestor Cram and Candace Schermerhorn. Northern Light Productions, 1997.

WEBSITES AND ORGANIZATIONS

A Call to Men: www.acalltomen.com

A Call to Men is an organization that works to eradicate both sexism and violence against women.

The American Association of University Women: http://aauw.org

The American Association of University Women advances equity for women and girls through advocacy, education, and research.

Bitch: Feminist Response to Pop Culture: http://bitchmagazine.org
Bitch is a print magazine devoted to critique and feminist analysis of pop culture, including TV, movies, magazines, advertising, and similar media outlets.

Byron Hurt: www.bhurt.com
Byron Hurt is an antisexist activist who provides cutting-edge male leadership, expert analysis, keynote addresses, and workshop facilitation in the field of sexual and gender violence prevention and education.

The Dad Man: http://thedadman.com
Launched by Joe Kelly, this website and blog focuses on media and marketing's impact on families; successful strategies for raising girls and boys; and how professionals can mobilize fathers as allies in their work.

Domestic Abuse Helpline for Men and Women: www.dahmw.info
The Domestic Abuse Helpline for Men and Women provides services and support for survivors of violence and their families.

Fem.Men.Ist: http://fem-men-ist.blogspot.com
Blog host and author Richard describes Fem.Men.Ist this way: "collaborative brainstorming and revolutionary heartstorming towards conscious community—race, gender, sexuality & masculinity politics, news, events, resources, personal perspectives and good conversations too."

Feministing.com: http://feministing.com
Feministing in an online blog focusing on issues affecting young women's lives and futures. Feministing provides a platform for young women to comment, analyze, influence and connect.

Gabe Kapler Foundation: www.kaplerfoundation.org
The Gabe Kapler Foundation is a family-led organization committed to ending domestic violence.

Gay Men's Domestic Violence Project: www.gmdvp.org
The Gay Men's Domestic Violence Project is an organization started by a gay male survivor of partner abuse. The organization advocates for nonviolence in the lives of gay men and offers support for those who have experienced abuse.

Gay Men's Health Crisis: www.gmhc.org/index.html
Gay Men's Health Crisis is a not-for-profit organization dedicated to eradicating AIDS in the United States.

Generation Five: www.generationfive.org
Generation Five is an organization devoted to ending child sexual abuse within the next five generations.

Hotlines: www.xris.com/survivor/msa/hotlines.html
This webpage provides hotline numbers and resources for male survivors of sexual assault. This list includes resources in the United States, Canada, and Europe.

Jackson Katz: www.jacksonkatz.com
Katz is one of America's leading male antisexist activists. He is the cofounder of the Mentors in Violence Prevention (MVP) program and the author of *The Macho Paradox*.

Jewish Male Survivors of Sexual Abuse: http://www.theawarenesscenter.org/mens.html
Jewish Male Survivors of Sexual Abuse is a resource page for Jewish men who have suffered from various forms of sexual abuse. This site includes articles, essays, links to other websites, and so forth.

Male Athletes Against Violence: www.umaine.edu/maav
Started by a University of Maine football player, this group of male athletes works to end violence against women.
Male Survivor: www.malesurvivor.org
Through support, advocacy, treatment, education, and activism, Male Survivor works to prevent, heal, and eliminate the sexual victimization of boys and men.

The Man Files: http://TheManFiles.wordpress.com
This group blog brings together a range of subjects, from sex to work to fashion to fatherhood, engaging scholars, bloggers, and readers in a popular online forum about what it means these days to "be a man."

The Masculinity Project: www.blackpublicmedia.org
The Masculinity Project gathers multigenerational voices to explore the question, What does it mean to be a man? With a focus on the black community in the twenty-first century, this multimedia resource provides video/audio playback, social networking, and community forums around important topics of justice, family, community, and culture.

Media Education Foundation: www.mediaed.org
The Media Education Foundation produces films that challenge American viewers and inspire dialogue on the social, political, and cultural implications of the media.

Men Against Sexual Violence: www.menagainstsexualviolence.org
Men Against Sexual Violence is a Pennsylvania-based group that organizes men to work against sexual violence and rape.

Men Against Violence: www.plu.edu/~mav
Men Against Violence is a student organization on the campus of Pacific Lutheran University in Tacoma, WA. Its mission is to educate the campus community how to live violence free and with respect for others.

Men Can Stop Rape: www.mencanstoprape.org
Men Can Stop Rape is an organization focused on encouraging male youth to challenge sexism in an effort to end sexual violence against women.

Meninist: www.feminist.com/resources/links/men.htm
Meninist is a worldwide organization of men who support feminism's goal of political, social, and economic equality for women.

The Men's Bibliography: http://mensbiblio.xyonline.net
The Men's Bibliography, compiled by scholar Michael Flood, provides links to writing on men, masculinity, gender, and sexuality.

Men's Health Network: www.menshealthnetwork.org
Men's Health Network provides men and their families with the tools and resources to live healthy lives.
Men's Leadership Project: http://mlp.virginia.edu
The Men's Leadership Project, based at the University of Virginia, educates men and boys of all ages to be responsible, ethical, gender-aware leaders.

Men's Resource Center for Change: www.mrcforchange.org
Men's Resource Center for Change supports and challenges men while developing men's leadership in eradicating individual, family, and community violence.

Men's Resources International: http://mensresourcesinternational.org
Men's Resources International is an international organization devoted to ending violence and creating more positive visions of masculinity.

Men Stopping Rape: http://danenet.wicip.org/msr
Men Stopping Rape is a Wisconsin-based organization of men working to challenge the culture of masculinity that leads to male violence.

Men Stopping Violence: www.menstoppingviolence.org
Men Stopping Violence works on local, national, and international levels to end men's violence against women.

Mentors in Violence Prevention (MVP): www.sportinsociety.org/vpd/mvp.php
MVP provides leadership training to student athletes and leaders to give them the tools to help end rape, battering, and sexual harassment.

National Association for Males with Eating Disorders: http://namedinc.org
This website provides information, links, and a toll-free hotline for men struggling with
eating disorders.

National Organization for Men Against Sexism (NOMAS): www.nomas.org
NOMAS is a pro-feminist, antiracist, and gay-affirmative organization dedicated to
improving men's lives.

One in Four: www.oneinfourusa.org
One in Four offers antirape training and education targeted primarily at all-male groups
at colleges, high schools, the military, and local community organizations.

Paul Kivel, Violence Prevention Educator: www.paulkivel.com
Kivel's work elaborates on the ways in which we can create sustainable, nurturing
communities.

Renaissance Male Project: http://renaissancemaleproject.com
The Renaissance Male Project is a multicultural organization committed to educating men
and boys on how to reach their full potential and become respectful partners of women.
Scenarios USA: http://scenariosusa.org/index.html
Scenarios USA is a nonprofit organization that produces films on various topics related
to masculinity. The films are made by young people for young people.

Tour for Equality: http://tour4equality.blogspot.com
The Tour for Equality was organized by a group of men riding their bikes across the
United States and through East Asia to educate people about women's rights and to
spread the message against violence against women.

2025 Campaign for Black Men and Boys: www.2025bmb.org
The 2025 Campaign is committed to creating a society in which African American men
and boys can confidently pursue their dreams and ambitions.

Voice Male magazine: www.voicemalemagazine.org
Voice Male is a male positive, pro-feminist magazine featuring current issues in gender
justice.

White Ribbon Campaign: www.whiteribbon.ca
Working in more than fifty-five countries, the White Ribbon Campaign educates men
and boys in an effort to end violence against women.

XY: Men, Masculinities, and Gender Politics: www.xyonline.net
XY is a space to explore issues of gender and sexuality and to engage in discussion about
personal and social change.

SOURCES

Chapter 1

Anzaldúa, Gloria. *Borderlands/La Frontera: The New Mestiza*. San Francisco: Spinsters/ Aunt Lute, 1987.

Arber, Brandon. "It's Just Common Sense," in Shira Tarrant, ed. *Men Speak Out: Views on Gender, Sex, and Power*. New York: Routledge, 2008, pp. 163–164.

Bindel, Julie. "The New Feminists." *Guardian*, Tuesday, November 28, 2006, p. 12.

Bortnichak, Greg. "The Starbucks Intervention," in Shira Tarrant, ed. *Men Speak Out: Views on Gender, Sex, and Power*. New York: Routledge, 2008, p. 147.

Carter, Derrais. "This Is What a Feminist Looks Like," in Shira Tarrant, ed. *Men Speak Out: Views on Gender, Sex, and Power*. New York: Routledge, 2008, p. 152.

Collins, Patricia Hill. "It's All in the Family: Intersections of Gender, Race and Nation." *Hypatia: A Journal of Feminist Philosophy*, vol. 13, no. 3 (1998), p. 68.

Crass, Chris. "How Can I Be Sexist? I'm an Anarchist!" in Shira Tarrant, ed. *Men Speak Out: Views on Gender, Sex, and Power*. New York: Routledge, 2008, p. 284.

Crenshaw, Kimberlé. "Demarginalizing the Intersection of Race and Sex: A Black Feminist Critique of Antidiscrimination Doctrine, Feminist Theory, and Antiracist Politics," in Katharine T. Bartlett and Rosanne Kennedy, eds. *Feminist Legal Theory: Readings in Law and Gender*. Boulder, CO: Westview, 1991.

Farrell, Warren with Steven Svoboda and James P. Sterba. *Does Feminism Discriminate Against Men?: A Debate*. New York: Oxford University, 2008, p. 12.

Flood, Michael. "Frequently Asked Questions About Pro-Feminist Men and Pro-Feminist Men's Politics." www.xyonline.net/misc/pffaq.html. Accessed June 23, 2008.

Gandhi, Nighat. "Can Men Be the Allies of Feminism?" www.xyonline.net /Canmenbeallies.shtml. Accessed June 23, 2008.

Grant, Judith. *Fundamental Feminism: Contesting the Core Concepts of Feminist Theory*. New York: Routledge, 1993, p. 109.

Guerrilla Girls. *Bitches, Bimbos and Ballbreakers: The Guerrilla Girls' Illustrated Guide to Female Stereotypes*. New York: Penguin, 2003, pp. 7–8.

Hamrick, Karen and Kristina J. Shelley. "How Much Time Do Americans Spend

Preparing and Eating Food?" www.ers.usda.gov/AmberWaves/November05 /DataFeature. Accessed December 31, 2008.

hooks, bell. *bell hooks: Cultural Criticism and Transformation*, Sut Jhally, dir. Northampton, MA: Media Education Foundation, 1997.

———. *Feminist Theory: From Margin to Center*. Cambridge, MA: South End, 2000, pp. 68 and 82.

Jensen, Robert. *Getting Off: Pornography and the End of Masculinity*. Cambridge, MA: South End, 2007, pp. 27, 29, and 31.

Jervis, Lisa and Andi Zeisler. "Barbie Can Just Bite Me." *Bitch: Feminist Response to Pop Culture*, vol. 1, no. 3 (1996), p. 7.

Katz, Jackson. *The Macho Paradox: Why Some Men Hurt Women and How All Men Can Help*. Naperville, IL: Sourcebooks, 2006, pp. 1–3, 15, and 16.

Kimmel, Michael S. "Who's Afraid of Men Doing Feminism?" in Tom Digby, ed. *Men Doing Feminism (Thinking Gender)*. New York: Routledge, 1998.

Labaton, Vivien and Dawn Lundy Martin, eds. *The Fire This Time: Young Activists and the New Feminism*. New York: Random House, 2004, p. xxiii.

Lasswell, Harold. *Politics: Who Gets What, When, How*. New York: McGraw-Hill, 1936.

Lyman, Peter. "The Fraternal Bond as a Joking Relationship: A Case Study of the Role of Sexist Jokes in Male Group Bonding," in Michael S. Kimmel and Michael A. Messner, eds. *Men's Lives*, 7th ed. San Francisco: Pearson, 2007, pp. 153–162.

Meninist: Men Supporting the Women's Movement. www.feminist.com/resources/links /men.htm. Accessed September 12, 2008.

Rape, Abuse and Incest National Network. www.rainn.org/statistics. Accessed November 1, 2008.

———. "The Offenders." http://rainn.org/get-information/statistics/sexual-assault -offenders. Accessed December 31, 2008.

Rupp, Leila J. "The Women's Community in the National Woman's Party, 1945 to the 1960s." *Signs*, vol. 10, no. 4 (1985), p. 722.

Schafer, Grantlin. "Breaking the Silence One Mile at a Time," in Shira Tarrant, ed. *Men Speak Out: Views on Gender, Sex, and Power*. New York: Routledge, 2008.

Shepherd, Matthew. "Feminism, Men, and the Study of Masculinity: Which Way Now?," in Steven P. Schacht and Doris W. Ewing, eds. *Feminism and Men: Reconstructing Gender Relations*. New York: New York University, 1998, p. 174.

Stryker, Susan. "(De)Subjugated Knowledge: An Introduction to Transgender Studies," in Susan Stryker and Stephen Whittle, eds. *The Transgender Studies Reader*. New York: Routledge, 2006, p. 7.

Swanbrow, Diane. "Study Finds American Men Doing More Housework." *The University Record*, March 25, 2002. www.ur.umich.edu/0102/Mar25_02/16.htm. Accessed August 11, 2008.

Tarrant, Shira, ed. *Men Speak Out: Views on Gender, Sex, and Power*. New York: Routledge, 2008.

———. *When Sex Became Gender*. New York: Routledge, 2006.

Weldon, S. L. "Rethinking Intersectionality: Some Conceptual Problems and Solutions for the Comparative Study of Welfare States." Unpublished paper delivered at the 2005 Annual Meeting of the American Political Science Association, Washington, DC, September 1–4, 2005.

Chapter 2

Abisaab, Malek and Rula Jurdi Abisaab. "A Century After Qasim Amin: Fictive Kinship and Historical Uses of 'Tahrir al-Mara.'" *aljadid,* vol. 8, no. 38 (Winter 2002). www .aljadid.com/features/ACenturyAfterQasimAmin.html. Accessed October 3, 2008.

Agonito, Rosemary. *History of Ideas on Woman.* New York: Perigee, 1977, p. 224.

Ahmed, Leila. *Women and Gender in Islam: Historical Roots of a Modern Debate.* New Haven, CT: Yale University, 1992.

Amin, Qasim. *The Liberation of Women* and *The New Woman: Two Documents in the History of Egyptian Feminism.* Translated by Samiha Sidhom Peterson. Cairo, Egypt: The American University in Cairo, 2000, p. ix.

Bart, Pauline B. "Review: Their Pleasure and Our Danger." *Contemporary Sociology,* vol. 15, no. 6 (November 1986), pp. 832–835.

Bebel, August. *Women and Socialism.* Translated by Meta L. Stern. New York: Socialist Literature Co., 1910.

Blackwell, Henry Brown and Lucy Stone. "Protest (1855)," in Michael S. Kimmel and Thomas E. Mosmiller, eds. *Against the Tide: Pro-Feminist Men in the United States, 1776–1990: A Documentary History.* Boston: Beacon, 1992, p. 330.

Bly, Robert. *Iron John.* Reading, MA: Addison-Wesley, 1990.

Cain, Joey. "Radical Faerie Statement." http://eniac.yak.net/shaggy/faerieinf.html. Accessed November 2, 2008.

DeFrain, John. "Abortion." *Macmillan Encyclopedia of Death and Dying,* 2003. http://findarticles.com/p/articles/mi_gx5214/is_2003/ai_n19132040/pg_ 1?tag=artBody;col1. Accessed July 21, 2008.

Dell, Floyd. "Feminism for Men (1917)," in Michael S. Kimmel and Thomas E. Mosmiller, eds. *Against the Tide: Pro-Feminist Men in the United States, 1776–1990: A Documentary History.* Boston: Beacon, 1992, pp. 361–364.

Douglass, Frederick. *My Bondage and My Freedom.* 1855. Reprint, New York: Arno, 1968, p. 473.

———. *The Life and Times of Frederick Douglass: As Published in 1881,* revised ed. North Chelmsford, MA: Courier Dover, 2003, p. 345.

Engels, Friedrich. "The Origin of the Family, Private Property and the State," in Robert C. Tucker, ed. *The Marx-Engels Reader,* 2nd ed. New York: W. W. Norton, 1978.

Flood, Michael. "What's Wrong with Fathers' Rights?" in Shira Tarrant, ed. *Men Speak Out: Views on Gender, Sex, and Power.* New York: Routledge, 2008, p. 214.

Guerrero, Práxedis. "The Woman (1910)," in Michael S. Kimmel and Thomas E. Mosmiller, eds. *Against the Tide: Pro-Feminist Men in the United States, 1776–1990: A Documentary History.* Boston: Beacon, 1992, pp. 316–317.

Hapgood, Hutchins. "Learning and Marriage (c. 1915)," in Michael S. Kimmel and Thomas E. Mosmiller, eds. *Against the Tide: Pro-Feminist Men in the United States,*

1776–1990: A Documentary History. Boston: Beacon, 1992, p. 360.

Henrie, William Jennings Bryan, D.O. "A New Look at Abortion (1966)," in Michael S. Kimmel and Thomas E. Mosmiller, eds. *Against the Tide: Pro-Feminist Men in the United States, 1776–1990: A Documentary History*. Boston: Beacon, 1992, pp. 433–434.

John, Angela V. and Claire Eustance, eds. *The Men's Share? Masculinities, Male Support and Women's Suffrage in Britain, 1890–1920*. New York: Routledge, 1997.

Keen, Sam. *Fire in the Belly: On Being a Man*. New York: Bantam, 1992.

Kimmel, Michael S. "Men's Responses to Feminism at the Turn of the Century." *Gender and Society*, vol. 1, no. 3 (September 1987), pp. 261–83.

———. *The History of Men: Essays on the History of American and British Masculinities*. Albany, NY: State University of New York, 2005, pp. 84–86.

Kimmel, Michael S. and Thomas E. Mosmiller, eds. *Against the Tide: Pro-Feminist Men in the United States, 1776–1990: A Documentary History*. Boston: Beacon, 1992, pp. xx and xxii.

Lange, Lynda. "The Function of Equal Education in Plato's *Republic*," in James P. Sterba, ed. *Social and Political Philosophy: Classical Western Texts in Feminist and Multicultural Perspectives*, 3rd ed. Belmont, CA: Wadsworth, 2003, pp. 33–40.

Lennon, John and Yoko Ono. "Women Is the "N" of the World." www.youtube.com /watch?v=S5lMxWWK218. Accessed July 16, 2008.

Mill, John Stuart. *On Liberty and Other Writings*, Stefan Collini, ed. New York: Cambridge University, 1989.

———. "The Subjection of Women," in Alice S. Rossi, ed. *The Feminist Papers: From Adams to de Beauvoir*. Boston: Northeastern University, 1973, p. 207.

Newton, Judith. *From Panthers to Promise Keepers: Rethinking the Men's Movement*. Lanham, MD: Rowman & Littlefield, 2005, p. 111.

National Organization for Men Against Sexism. "Tenets." www.nomas.org/tenets. Accessed October 6, 2008.

O'Neill, William L., ed. *Echoes of Revolt: The Masses, 1911–1917*. Chicago: Quadrangle, 1966, p. 21.

Owen, Robert Dale. "Marriage Contract with Mary Jane Robinson (1832)," in Michael S. Kimmel and Thomas E. Mosmiller, eds. *Against the Tide: Pro-Feminist Men in the United States, 1776–1990: A Documentary History*. Boston: Beacon, 1992, p. 75.

Plato. *The Republic*, in James P. Sterba, ed. *Social and Political Philosophy: Classical Western Texts in Feminist and Multicultural Perspectives*, 3rd ed. Belmont, CA: Wadsworth, 2003, pp. 24, 25, and 28.

Rossi, Alice S., ed. *The Feminist Papers: From Adams to de Beauvoir*. Boston: Northeastern University, 1973, p. 473.

Salaam, Kalamu ya. "The Struggle to Smash Sexism Is a Struggle to Develop Women (1980)," in Michael S. Kimmel and Thomas E. Mosmiller, eds. *Against the Tide: Pro-Feminist Men in the United States, 1776–1990: A Documentary History*. Boston: Beacon, 1992, p. 443.

Snodgrass, Jon, ed. *A Book of Readings: For Men Against Sexism*. Albion, CA: Times Change, 1977.

Stenberg, Kim Yoonok. "Review: *The Men's Share? Masculinities, Male Support and Women's Suffrage in Britain, 1890–1920*, Angela V. John and Claire Eustance, eds." *Albion: A Quarterly Journal Concerned with British Studies*, vol. 30, no. 3 (Autumn 1998), p. 549.

Stoltenberg, John. "Why I Stopped Trying to Be a Real Man." http://web.archive.org /web/20070402172337/http://www.feminista.com/archives/v1n2/stoltenberg.html. Accessed October 6, 2008.

Trimberger, Ellen Kay. "Feminism, Men, and Modern Love: Greenwich Village 1900–1925," in Ann Snitow, Christine Stansell, and Sharon Thompson, eds. *Powers of Desire: The Politics of Sexuality*. New York: Monthly Review, 1983.

Weld, Theodore D. "Man's Disparagement of Woman in All Times and Climes (1855?)," in Michael S. Kimmel and Thomas E. Mosmiller, eds. *Against the Tide: Pro-Feminist Men in the United States, 1776–1990: A Documentary History*. Boston: Beacon, 1992, pp. 297–299.

Whittle, Stephen. Foreword in Susan Stryker and Stephen Whittle, eds. *The Transgender Studies Reader*. New York: Routledge, 2006, pp. xii–xiii.

Willis, Andrew. "Band of Brothers: Antisexism in the Punk Movement." *Bitch: Feminist Response to Pop Culture*, Issue 28, Spring 2005, p. 50.

Wittman, Carl. "A Gay Manifesto (1972)," in Michael S. Kimmel and Thomas E. Mosmiller, eds. *Against the Tide: Pro-Feminist Men in the United States, 1776–1990: A Documentary History*. Boston: Beacon, 1992, p. 442.

Chapter 3

Armengol, Josep M. "Gendering Men: Re-Visions of Violence as a Test of Manhood in American Literature." *Atlantis*, vol. 29, no. 2 (December 2007), pp. 75–92. www .atlantisjournal.org/Papers/29_2/JosepMArmengol2007.pdf. Accessed October 31, 2008.

Beauvoir, Simone de. *The Second Sex*, Translated by H. M. Parshley. New York: Vintage, [1952] 1989.

Bell, Chris, dir. *Bigger, Stronger, Faster*: Is It Still Cheating If Everyone's Doing It?* BSF Film, 2008. www.biggerstrongerfastermovie.com. Accessed June 26, 2008.

Bem, Sandra Lipsitz. "The Measurement of Psychological Androgyny." *Journal of Consulting and Clinical Psychology*, vol. 42 (1974), pp. 155–162.

Berkowitz, Gale. "UCLA Study on Friendship Among Women: An Alternative to Fight or Flight." www.anapsid.org/cnd/gender/tendfend.html. Accessed December 26, 2008.

Bodner, Allen. *When Boxing Was a Jewish Sport*. Westport, CT: Praeger Trade, 1997.

Brannon, Robert and Deborah David. *The Forty-Nine Percent Majority*. Reading, MA: Addison-Wesley, 1976.

Britt, Robert Roy. "Study: Men Hard-Wired to Ignore Their Wives." February 15, 2007. www.foxnews.com/story/0,2933,251966,00.html. Accessed December 26, 2008.

Capraro, Rocco L. "Why College Men Drink: Alcohol, Adventure and the Paradox of Masculinity," in Michael S. Kimmel and Michael A. Messner, eds. *Men's Lives*. 7th ed. San Francisco: Pearson, 2007, pp. 182–195.

Catalyst, Clint. Personal correspondence. September 8, 2008.

Chandler, Michael Alison and Maria Glod. "More Schools Trying Separation of the Sexes." *Washington Post*, Sunday, June 15, 2008, p. A01.

Chaudhry, Lakshmi. "Men Growing Up to Be Boys: Madison Avenue Cultivates a Peter Pan Version of Masculinity." *In These Times*, March 17, 2006. www.inthesetimes.com /article/2526, p. 1. Accessed June 16, 2008.

Cintron, L. G. "Attitudes Towards Work and Family Balance Across Generational Groupings." Paper presented at the annual meeting of the American Sociological Association, Atlanta Hilton Hotel, Atlanta, GA, August 16, 2003.

Connell, R. W. *Masculinities*. 2nd ed. Berkeley: University of California, 2005.

Creighton, Allan and Paul Kivel. *Helping Teens Stop Violence*. Alameda, CA: Hunter House, 1992.

Degler, Carl N. *In Search of Human Nature: The Decline and Revival of Darwinism in American Social Thought*. New York: Oxford University, 1991.

Denby, David. "A Fine Romance: The New Comedy of the Sexes." *The New Yorker*, July 23, 2007. www.newyorker.com/reporting/2007/07/23/070723fa_fact_denby. Accessed December 27, 2008.

Dokoupil, Tony. "Why I Am Leaving Guyland." *Newsweek*, August 30, 2008. www .newsweek.com/id/156372. Accessed November 2, 2008.

Fausto-Sterling, Anne. "That Sexe Which Prevaileth," in Rachel Adams and David Sauran, eds. *The Masculinity Studies Reader*. New York: Blackwell, 2002.

Freedman, David H. "The Aggressive Egg," *Discover*, June 1, 1992. http:// discovermagazine.com/1992/jun/theaggressiveegg55. Accessed June 16, 2008.

Gilder, George. *Men and Marriage*. Gretna, LA: Pelican, 1992.

Halberstam, Judith. "An Introduction to Female Masculinity: Masculinity Without Men," in Rachel Adams and David Savran, eds. *The Masculinity Studies Reader*. Malden, MA: Blackwell, 2006, pp. 355–374.

Holmes, Betty. "WIN Wyoming: Thought Bullets for December 2001: 40 Years of GI Joe." www.uwyo.edu/winwyoming/bullets/2001/bullets12-01.htm. Accessed October 31, 2008.

hooks, bell. *The Will to Change: Men, Masculinity, and Love*. New York: Atria, 2004.

Hopkinson, Natalie and Natalie Y. Moore. *Deconstructing Tyrone: A New Look at Black Masculinity in the Hip-Hop Generation*. San Francisco: Cleis, 2006, p. xii.

Hurt, Byron. "Hip-Hop: Beyond Beats and Rhymes," in Bill Yousman, *Media Education Foundation Study Guide*. www.mediaed.org/wp/study-guides#G-I. Accessed November 2, 2008.

Katz, Jackson. *The Macho Paradox: Why Some Men Hurt Women and How All Men Can Help*. Naperville, IL: Sourcebooks, 2006.

Kimmel, Michael S. "Masculinity as Homophobia: Fear, Shame, and Silence in the Construction of Gender Identity," in Maurianne Adams, Warren J. Blumenfeld, Rosie

Castaneda, et al., eds. *Readings for Diversity and Social Justice: An Anthology on Racism, Antisemitism, Sexism, Heterosexism, Ableism, and Classism*. New York: Routledge, 2000, p. 215.

―――. *Guyland: The Perilous World Where Boys Become Men*. New York: HarperCollins, 2008.

Kimmel, Michael S. and Michael A. Messner, eds. *Men's Lives*, 7th ed. San Francisco: Pearson, 2007, pp. xv–xxiii.

King, Martin Luther, Jr. *Strength to Love*. Philadelphia: Fortress, 1981, p. 35.

Loe, Meika. "Fixing Broken Masculinity: Viagra as a Technology for the Production of Gender and Sexuality," in Michael S. Kimmel and Michael A. Messner, eds. *Men's Lives*, 7th ed. San Francisco: Pearson, 2007.

Lorber, Judith. "'Night to His Day': The Social Construction of Gender," in Maurianne Adams, Warren J. Blumenfeld, Rosie Castaneda, et al., eds. *Readings for Diversity and Social Justice: An Anthology on Racism, Antisemitism, Sexism, Heterosexism, Ableism, and Classism*. New York: Routledge, 2000, p. 205.

McCaughey, Martha. *The Caveman Mystique: Pop-Darwinism and the Debates Over Sex, Violence, and Science*. New York: Routledge, 2008, pp. 2, 3, 7, and 23.

Mead, Margaret. *Sex and Temperament in Three Primitive Societies*. New York: W. Morrow, 1935.

Messner, Michael A. *Taking the Field: Women, Men, and Sports*. Minneapolis: University of Minnesota, 2002.

Mirandé, Alfredo. *Hombres y Machos: Masculinity and Latino Culture*. Boulder, CO: Westview, 1997, p. 67.

Paoletti, Jo B. "Clothing and Gender in America: Children's Fashions, 1890–1920." *Signs*, vol. 13, no. 1 (Autumn 1987), pp. 136–143.

Pascoe, C. J. *Dude, You're a Fag: Masculinity and Sexuality in High School*. Berkeley: University of California, 2007, p. 116.

Rhoads, Steven E. *Taking Sex Differences Seriously*. San Francisco: Encounter, 2004.

Rodriguez, Luis J. "On Macho," in Ray González, ed. *Muy Macho: Latino Men Confront Their Manhood*. New York: Anchor, 1996, pp. 193 and 195.

Savoie, Keely. "WIMN's Voices: A Group Blog on Women, Media, AND . . ." www.wimnonline.org/WIMNsVoicesBlog/?author=41&profile#bio. Accessed August 29, 2008.

Sedgwick, Eve Kosofsky. "Gosh, Boy George, You Must Be Awfully Secure in Your Masculinity!," in eds. Maurice Berger, Brian Wallis, and Simon Watson *Constructing Masculinity*. New York: Routledge, 1995.

Sheets, Annamarie. "Has Feminism Changed Science? A Biological Perspective." www.mit.edu/~womens-studies/writingPrize/as03.html. Accessed October 17, 2008.

Stryker, Susan. *Transgender History*. Berkeley, CA: Seal, 2008, p. 4.

Tarrant, Shira, ed. *Men Speak Out: Views on Gender, Sex, and Power*. New York: Routledge, 2008, pp. 9 and 10.

Zerbisias, Antonia. "Biological Paradox: Men Hardwired to Be Extreme." March 5, 2008. www.thestar.com/comment/columnists/article/309294. Accessed December 26, 2008.

Chapter 4

Anderson-Minshall, Jacob. Personal correspondence. July 16, 2008.

Atherton-Zeman, Ben. Personal correspondence. July 16, 2008.

Darkness to Light. www.darkness2light.org/KnowAbout/articles_men_victims.asp. Accessed October 16, 2008.

Deutsch, Barry. "Male Privilege: Unpacking Men's Invisible Knapsack." *Voice Male*, (Summer 2008), pp. 12–14.

Firestone, Shulamith. *The Dialectic of Sex: The Case for Feminist Revolution*. New York: William Morrow, 1970.

Flood, Michael. "What's Wrong with Fathers' Rights?" in Shira Tarrant, ed. *Men Speak Out: Views on Gender, Sex, and Power*. New York: Routledge, 2008, p. 218.

Freiss, Steve. "More Men Taking Wives' Last Names," *USA Today*, March 21, 2007. www.usatoday.com/news/nation/2007-03-20-names-marriage_N.htm. Accessed June 26, 2008.

hooks, bell. *Feminist Theory: From Margin to Center*. Cambridge, MA: South End, 2000.

Human Rights Watch. "United States—Punishment and Prejudice: Racial Disparities in the War on Drugs: Incarceration and Race." www.hrw.org/reports/2000/usa /Rcedrg00-01.htm. Accessed October 10, 2008.

Jensen, Robert. *Getting Off: Pornography and the End of Masculinity*. Cambridge, MA: South End, 2007, pp. 48–49.

———. "Does Porn Make the Man?" www.alternet.org/story/67465. Accessed October 17, 2008.

Jhally, Sut, dir. *Dreamworlds 3: Desire, Sex, and Power in Music Video*. Media Education Foundation, 2007.

Kailey, Matt. Personal correspondence. July 18, 2008.

Katz, Jackson. *The Macho Paradox: Why Some Men Hurt Women and How All Men Can Help*. Naperville, IL: Sourcebooks, 2006, pp. 91 and 111.

Kivel, Paul. *Men's Work: How to Stop the Violence That Tears Our Lives Apart*. Center City, MN: Hazelden, 1998.

Lyman, Peter. "The Fraternal Bond as a Joking Relationship: A Case Study of the Role of Sexist Jokes in Male Group Bonding," in Michael S. Kimmel and Michael A. Messner, eds. *Men's Lives*, 7th ed. San Francisco: Pearson, 2007, pp. 153–162.

Males, Mike. "The Real Mistake in 'Teen Pregnancy.'" *Los Angeles Times*, Sunday, July 13, 2008, p. M6.

Marcuse, Herbert. *One-Dimensional Man*. New York: Routledge, [1964] 2006.

McIntosh, Peggy. "White Privilege: Unpacking the Invisible Knapsack." http://seamonkey .ed.asu.edu/~mcisaac/emc598ge/Unpacking.html. Accessed October 17, 2008.

Men Can Stop Rape. http://www.mencanstoprape.org. Accessed October 17, 2008.

Men's Resources International. "Beliefs About Men." www.mensresourcesinternational .org/documents/Beliefs_About_Men.pdf. Accessed October 17, 2008.

Miedzian, Myriam. *Boys Will Be Boys: Breaking the Link Between Masculinity and Violence*. New York: Lantern, 2002, pp. 3 and 4.

National Coalition Against Violent Athletes, www.ncava.org/ncavamain.html. Accessed December 31, 2008.

Rape, Abuse and Incest National Network. www.rainn.org/statistics. Accessed November 1, 2008.

Ruby, Jennie. "The Grammar of Male Violence." *off our backs*, vol. xxxiv, no. 9/10, (September–October 2004), p. 26.

Serjeant, Jill. "Los Angeles Man Wins Right to Use Wife's Last Name." *Reuters*, May 5, 2008. www.reuters.com/article/lifestyleMolt/idUSN0541896320080505?feedType=RSS&feedName=lifestyleMolt&pageNumber=1&virtualBrandChannel=0. Accessed October 17, 2008.

Sessions Stepp, Laura. "A New Kind of Date Rape." *Cosmopolitan* (September 2007). www.cosmopolitan.com/sex-love/sex/new-kind-of-date-rape. Accessed October 17, 2008.

Shaw, Hank. *It's Time for Guys to Put an End to This*. Rochester, NY: Hank Shaw, 2000.

Smith, Lauren. http://jadedhippy.blogspot.com/2008/07/kyriarchy.html. Accessed October 17, 2008.

U.S. Department of Justice. Bureau of Justice Statistics, Prison Statistics. www.ojp.usdoj.gov/bjs/prisons.htm. Accessed October 17, 2008.

Woods, Jewel. "The Black Male Privileges Checklist." Renaissance Male Project, 2008. http://jewelwoods.com/node/9. Accessed September 8, 2008.

Chapter 5

Cleaver, Frances, ed. *Masculinities Matter! Men, Gender and Development*. London: Zed, 2003, p. xii.

Daddy Dialectic. http://daddy-dialectic.blogspot.com. Accessed September 10, 2008.

Different Kind of Dude Fest. http://differentkindofdudefest.dead-city.org. Accessed September 10, 2008.

Elliott, Christopher L. Wilcox. Personal correspondence. August 22, 2008.

Ending Violence Against Women: Making It Happen in Los Angeles. Policy Summit, March 12, 2008.

Flood, Michael. "Involving Men in Efforts to End Violence Against Women." Domestic Violence Network Forum (Eastern Suburbs Domestic Violence Network), March 18, 2008, Sydney, Australia. www.xyonline.net. Accessed September 10, 2008.

Fem-Men-Ist. http://fem-men-ist.blogspot.com. Accessed October 17, 2008.

Gandhi, Nighat. "Can Men Be the Allies of Feminism?" www.xyonline.net/Canmenbeallies.shtml. Accessed October 17, 2008.

hooks, bell. *Feminist Theory: From Margin to Center*. Cambridge, MA: South End, 2000, p. 73.

Katz, Jackson. http://jacksonkatz.com. Accessed June 12, 2008.

———. "Ten Things Men Can Do to Prevent Gender Violence." Jackson Katz, 1999. http://jacksonkatz.com/wmcd.html. Accessed June 12, 2008.

Kendall, Frances E. "How to Be an Ally if You Are a Person with Privilege." www.scn.org/friends/ally.html. Accessed October 17, 2008.

Law, Ian. "Adopting the Principle of Pro-Feminism," in Maurianne Adams, Warren J. Blumenfeld, Rosie Castaneda, et al., eds. *Readings for Diversity and Social Justice: An Anthology on Racism, Antisemitism, Sexism, Heterosexism, Ableism, and Classism*. New York: Routledge, 2000, pp. 254–255.

Meier, Dani. Personal correspondence. August 30, 2008.

Men Against Violence. "Mission Statement." http://wrc.ua.edu/involved/mav.htm. Accessed December 10, 2008.

National Criminal Justice Reference Service. "Trafficking in Persons—Facts and Figures." www.ncjrs.gov/spotlight/trafficking/facts.html. Accessed January 2, 2009.

National Organization for Men Against Sexism. www.nomas.org. Accessed October 17, 2008.

Okun, Rob. "Double Play: Gabe and Lisa Kapler Take the Field Against Domestic Violence." *Voice Male* (Fall 2005), pp. 8–9, 16, 26.

———. "A Call to Men: From Bystanders to Activists." *Voice Male* (Fall 2005), p. 2.

One In Four. http://oneinfourusa.org. Accessed October 17, 2008.

Perez, Rob. "Men Speak Out About Rise in Domestic Abuse." *Honolulu Advertiser*, August 2, 2008.

Poole, Jay. "Good Ol' Boy: A Tale of Transformation in the Rural South," in Shira Tarrant, ed. *Men Speak Out: Views on Gender, Sex, and Power*. New York: Routledge, 2008, pp. 272–275.

Porter, Tony and Ted Bunch. "A Call to Men." *Voice Male* (Fall 2006), p. 10.

Porter, Tony, Brenda Ross, and Ted Bunch. "10 Things Men Can Do to End Violence Against Women." A Call to Men: The National Association of Men and Women Committed to Ending Violence Against Women. Pomona, NY, 2005.

Rebeldad. www.rebeldad.com. Accessed October 17, 2008.

Renaissance Male Project. http://renaissancemaleproject.com. Accessed January 2, 2009.

Ruddy, Jenn. "Gender Mending: Men, Masculinity, and Feminism." www.xyonline.net /Gendermending.shtml. Accessed October 17, 2008.

Schafer, Grantlin. "Breaking the Silence One Mile at a Time," in Shira Tarrant, ed. *Men Speak Out: Views on Gender, Sex, and Power*. New York: Routledge, 2008, pp. 261–263.

Shaw, Hank. *Stand-Up Guys No. 1*. Rochester, NY: Hank Shaw, 2008.

Smith, Jeremy Adam. "Playground Vertigo," in Shira Tarrant, ed. *Men Speak Out: Views on Gender, Sex, and Power*. New York: Routledge, 2008, p. 203.

———. *The Daddy Shift: How Stay-at-Home Fathers, Breadwinning Mothers, and Shared Parenting Are Transforming the Twenty-First-Century Family*. Beacon, 2009.

Standifer, Cid. "Riverview Talks Strippers and 'Real Men.'" *Galena Gazette*, December 18, 2007. www.galenagazette.com/main.asp?SectionID=142&SubSectionID=344& ArticleID=11210&TM=36524.05. Accessed December 27, 2008.

Steinem, Gloria. "Revving Up for the Next Twenty-Five Years," in Maurianne Adams, Warren J. Blumenfeld, Rosie Castaneda, et al., eds. *Readings for Diversity and Social Justice: An Anthology on Racism, Antisemitism, Sexism, Heterosexism, Ableism, and*

Classism. New York: Routledge, 2000, p. 257.

U.N. Expert Group on Role of Men, Boys in Achieving Gender Equality. www.un.org /News/Press/docs/2003/dev2442.doc.htm. Accessed October 17, 2008.

Woods, Jewel. "The Black Male Privileges Checklist." Renaissance Male Project, 2008. http://jewelwoods.com/node/9. Accessed September 8, 2008.

INDEX

40–41; history of 29–33; men against 54; racial intersectionality within 13–14; as relevant to men 15–18; as a social justice movement 57–58; stereotyping 22, 23; terminology of 23–25; trans activism and 57; by women of color 24

"Feminism, Men, and the Study of Masculinity" (Shepherd): 15

feminist.com: 24

feministing.com: 124

feminists, male: in the British women's movement 36–37; campus/community activism by 124–130; challenges facing 1, 2, 21; encouraging 119–120; gay 51; historic 30–31; incongruities in the work of 53–54; in-home work by 140–142; international 28, 33, 44–45; male suffragists 34, 37; national/global activism by 120–124; self-identified 24; at the Seneca Falls Convention 34, 35, 38; statements from 132–133; stereotyping 23; unlabeled 23

Feminist Theory: From Margin to Center (hooks): 18, 120

Fem-Men-Ist: 135

Filmspotting: 99

Fire in the Belly: On Being a Man (Keen): 55

Firestone, Shulamith: 94

The Fire This Time: Young Activists and the New Feminism (Labaton and Martin): 3

first wave feminism: 29

"Fixing Broken Masculinity: Viagra as a Technology for the Production of Gender and Sexuality" (Loe): 79

Flood, Michael: on antisexist men 24; on community activism 124; on father's rights movements 56,

113; on male privilege 116; on violence intervention 143

Food Not Bombs: 18

Frank, Brian: 134

Franti, Michael: 135

"The Fraternal Bond as a Joking Relationship" (Lyman): 22, 106

fraternities: 12

Freedman, David H.: 68

"free love": 43–46, 47

free speech movement: 29

Freeze, Bishop: 135, 136

Friess, Steve: 98

From Panthers to Promise Keepers (Newton): 50

Fundamental Feminism (Grant): 15

G

Gabe Kapler Foundation: 125

Gandhi, Mahatma: 87

Gandhi, Nighat: 3, 18–19, 141

Garrison, William Lloyd: 38

gay activism: 136–137

Gay Men's Domestic Violence Project (GMDVP): 136–137

gender: activism against binary 57; assumptions, biased 94; binary essentialism 16; color-coding 59–60; discrimination 131; feminism as questioning 3, 11; as "hardwired" 71; as learned 6–7, 59; legislating 77; maneuvering 75; as non-binary 72–77; normalizing 8, 70–71; pop culture as school for 7–8; privilege of ignoring 92; sperm-and-egg rhetoric 67–69; trans and queer 57–58, 74

"Gender Mending: Men, Masculinity, and Feminism" (Ruddy): 146

genderqueer movements: 57–58, 136–137

Gender Violence Institute: 116

neutrality, gendering: 95, 100
Nevinson, Henry: 37
New Left: 49
Newton, Judith: 50, 55
The New Woman (Al-Mar'a al-jadida)
(Amin): 45
"Night to His Day" (Lorber): 74
Nomenus Wolf Creek Radical Faerie
Sanctuary: 51
"normal": 70
North Star: 35

O

Okun, Rob: 142
O'Neill, William: 43
One in Four: 2, 137, 144
"On Macho" (Rodriguez): 87
Ono, Yoko: 50
opportunity: custom as denying 33;
equal 3, 4; gender-dependent 6, 11
oppression: economics of 40; of men
28, 113; politics of 14; Weld on 42
*Origin of the Family, Private Property
and the State* (Engels): 40
Owen, Robert Dale: 39, 42, 46
OXFAM International: 120

P

Paoletti, Jo: 60
parental alienation theory: 56
Pascoe, C. J.: 75, 79
passivity, female: 72
passivity, male: 5
patriarchy: challenges to men within
14, 28; vs. kyriarchy 108; and
marriage contracts 98
Peace over Violence: 104
Penelope, Julie: 100
"The Personal is Political": 8, 10,
12, 50
Phelps, Michael: 69
Phillips, Wendell: 34
physique, male: 79–80

Pill, the: 47
Pillsbury, Parker: 38
Plato: 28, 30
play, children's: 94
pleasure, sexual: 102
politics: of the founding fathers 27;
of men's groups 56; 1960s radical
49; "The Personal is Political"
8–13, 50; sexual 47
Poole, Jay: 130–131
pop culture: creating literacy in
134–136; gender training 7–8;
masculinity in 80–81; music videos
98
pornography: 102–104
Porter, Tony: 137, 144
power: gendered 87; in the margins
112; perceived as a limited resource
20; and powerlessness 84, 108; and
privilege 80, 92; and sexist joking
106–107
powerlessness: 84, 108
pregnancy, teen: 101
prevention: 19
privilege, male: 89–117; black
90–91, 127; checklist 96–97;
confronting 112–117; courage
to address 93–94; unequal
107–112; linguistics of 99–102;
men reflect on 110–111; and
pornography 102–104; power and
80; relinquishing 114, 115; white
91–92
Program H: 124
protectionism, gender: 17–18, 37
Purvis, Robert: 34

R

racial issues: arrest statistics 91;
in the birth control movement
47; black male privilege 89–90,
127; confronting assumptions 2;
intersectionality 13–14, 53; in rape

statistics 10; stereotyping ethnicity 62, 81; in U.S. foundational politics 27; white privilege 91–92; in the women's movement 50
racism: 50, 107
Radcliffe Public Policy Center: 86
Radical Faeries: 51
rape: gray rape 105; marital 36, 39; of men and boys 91; men's freedom from fear of 94; men's help preventing 125–127; men's understanding of 104; preventing 136–140; statistics 10, 90
Real MEN's Project (Men Embracing Non-Violence): 125, 126, 143
Rebeldad: 135–136
Redmond, Charles: 34
Reform Bill (1867): 37
Reid, Brian: 135–136
Reitman, Ben: 54
Renaissance Male Project: 125
reproduction story, gendering the: 67–69
reproductive rights: activism protecting 146; history of 46–49; linguistic shape shifting and 101; male advocates of 16, 46; protests for 48; third wave feminism as aiding 32
The Republic (Plato): 30
Rhoads, Steven: 71
Rini, Dave: 145
rites of passage: 54
Riverview Center: 127
Rodrigues Jr., Richard: 148–149
Rodriguez, Luis J.: 87
Roe v. Wade: 146
Rogue Trooper: 7
role models: 124–125
role strain: 85
Rosenbaum, Mark: 99
Ross, Brenda: 137

Rossi, Alice: 40
Ruby, Jennie: 101
Ruddy, Jenn: 131, 146
Rupp, Leila: 24

S

Sadker, David: 71
Safe Passage: 125
Salaam, Kalamu ya: 53
San Francisco Conference on Abortion and Human Rights (1966): 49
Sanger, Margaret: 46, 47
Savoie, Keely: 67
Sax, Leonard: 71
Schafer, Grantlin: 18, 138, 144
Schivley, Christopher: 5
Schüssler Fiorenza. Elisabeth: 108–109
science: vs. fact 67, 69, 71; gender myths in 67–70
The Second Sex (de Beauvoir): 77
second wave feminism: 29, 54
Sedgewick, Eve Kosofsky: 75
Seneca Falls Convention: 34
separatism, male/female: 54
Serjeant, Jill: 99
sex: biological 6; male statistics 86; masculine right to 90–91; outside marriage 43–46; and politics 102
Sex and Temperament (Mead): 74
Sexing the Body: Gender Politics and the Construction of Sexuality (Fausto-Sterling): 76
sexism: confronting 1, 18, 28, 130–134; humorous 22, 104–107; John Lennon on 50; linguistic 99–102, 139; male bonding via 78, 106; and male privilege 93; men's groups against 51, 52; in radical politics 49; as root of violence 137
sexual assault: biologically explained 72, 73; of children 108; failure

U

United Nations: 120
University of Michigan Institute for Social Research: 9
"Unpacking Men's Invisible Knapsack" (Deutsch): 98

V

Van Hallgren, Sam: 99
veterans: 146
Viagra: 79
violence: biological explanation for 72, 73; cultural roots for 87; in fathers 56–57; as gender biased 10; gender-neutralizing 100–101; intervening vs. ignoring 142–145; men against 18; preventing 125–127, 136–140; in sports culture 82; statistics 19, 140
Violence Against Women Act (VAWA): 122

W

Walk a Mile in Her Shoes: 93
war, masculinity and: 122
weakness: 81
Webb, Marilyn Salzman: 49
Weld, Theodore Dwight: 42
Weldon, S. L.: 13
When Boxing Was a Jewish Sport (Bodner): 62
"White Privilege: Unpacking the Invisible Knapsack" (McIntosh): 89

White Ribbon Campaign: 17, 128
white supremacy: 130
Whittle, Stephen: 57
"Who's Afraid of Men Doing Feminism?" (Kimmel): 15
"Why College Men Drink: Alcohol, Adventure and the Paradox of Masculinity" (Capraro): 84
"Why I Stopped Trying to Be a Real Man" (Stoltenberg): 52–53
Willis, Andrew: 55
winning: 62–63
Wittman, Carl: 51
wives, legal rights for: 36–37
"The Woman" (Guerrero): 33
womanism: 24
women: awareness of gender in 92; of color 24, 50
Women and Socialism (Bebel): 41
women-only groups: 54
women's bodies: as arena of men's will 12, 98; control over 79; personal vigilance to 92
women's rights movement: 10, 35–37, 49, 50, 92
Woods, Jewel: 89, 97, 127

X

xaniths: 74

Y

Young Lions Program: 54

ACKNOWLEDGMENTS

While I hope *Men and Feminism* helps start (or continue) conversations about masculinity and gender equity, it owes a great deal to the scholarship and support of those who have gone before and to those who walk beside me in this venture. I lean on some and stand on the shoulders of others.

Chapter 2 relies heavily on the work of Michael Kimmel and Michael Mosmiller. My appreciation to both for their scholarship. Ongoing conversations with Jackson Katz honed my thinking about many of the issues reflected in this book. My students past and present have been wonderful sources of insight. Their enthusiasm and interest in changing the world continue to teach me well. My students from California State University, Long Beach, were amazing in hashing out a lot of the ideas in this book with me, especially those who took my class on masculinities in Fall 2007 and my political theory students from Fall 2008.

Special thanks go to Ashleigh Klein, Katie Sipes, Megan Adams, Shelby Woods, and Emma Douglas. Each is an amazing scholar-activist; all are in the classrooms and on the streets making a difference. These five get my hearty thanks for help with research and for our conversations about improving relationships and preventing violence and sexual assault.

Sometimes people come into our lives (or back into our lives) for reasons and with good timing. Karen Morgaine deserves credit for putting up with some quirky (and I hope charming) habits, erratic hours, and weird distractions while I was writing this book. And thanks to Micky Hohl for friendship, good food, and for helping me think through important questions that found their way into the pages of this book.

Deep love to Shawna Kenney, Renee Cramer, Jen Reed, Lana Haddad, Marjorie Jolles, and Hayley Miller for their professional encouragement and valuable friendship. I am fortunate to have friends who can talk about hegemony, politics, fashion, and Facebook in the same breath and with equal enthusiasm. With her smiles and sweetness, Eloise Miller provided lovingkindness without ever saying a word.

Judith Grant, Jan Simon, Wendy Griffin, Maggie Munoz, Beth Krumholz, Agathi Glezakos, Ann Meyers and Greg Meyers, Michael Perrick, and Didi Gerlach made themselves extra available during an extra-challenging year. The College of Liberal Arts at CSULB provided generous grant funding for scholarly and creative activities that helped smooth the creation of this book. Thank you.

This book is possible in the first place because Brooke Warner at Seal Press saw the importance of including it in the Seal Studies series. I appreciate her enthusiasm for the project. Jennie Goode has been an amazing, hands-on editor who knows her politics and feminist theory, and who can spot a clunky phrase from a mile away. This book would not be what it is without her keen eye. Stephanie Malinowski was an extraordinary intern. I appreciate her comments and insight on content and her help at the eleventh hour. Quinci Harris did amazing legwork tracking down images and securing permissions. Copy editor and proofreader Karen Bleske provided a sharp sense of detail. Finally, by sharing in the experience of a writer's joys and challenges, Jillian Lauren, Deborah Siegel, and Elline Lipkin have provided tremendous support. I hope I offer the same.

I appreciate the many friends, family members, and colleagues who remain unnamed, yet who helped to create safe psychic space. This helped me sit down and write.

All good love to my family, Mark and Judy Feingold, Sara Pollak, Alisa Feingold, David Feingold, Rachel Feingold and Gabriella, Jacob, Serena, and Jesse. My deepest love and eternal hugs and kisses are for my beautiful, wise, unique, and grounded daughter, Emilie Tarrant.

ABOUT THE AUTHOR

SHIRA TARRANT, PhD, is an expert in masculinities, feminist theory, and pop culture. She is the author of *When Sex Became Gender* (Routledge 2006), editor of the provocative anthology *Men Speak Out: Views on Gender, Sex, and Power* (Routledge 2008), and coeditor of *Fashion Talks: Undressing the Power of Style* (forthcoming). Her work has appeared in *Bitch, off our backs, Women's Studies Quarterly, Genre* magazine, and *The Women's Movement Today: An Encyclopedia of Third-Wave Feminism*, and on the popular blog *Girl with Pen.*

© Carlos Batts

Tarrant is a frequent speaker at college campuses and other public venues. She has been quoted widely in print, television, radio, and online media on the subject of gender politics. She received her PhD in political science from the University of California, Los Angeles, and is an assistant professor of women's studies at California State University, Long Beach. To read more about her work, see http://shiratarrant.com.

CREDITS

Chapter 1

Excerpt from "This Is What a Feminist Looks Like," by Derrais Carter, found in *Men Speak Out: Views on Gender, Sex, and Power,* edited by Shira Tarrant. (c) 2008. Reprinted by permission of Routledge.

"A Man's Work Is Never Done" cartoon provided by and reprinted with the permission of Nicholson. (c) 2003 Nicholson.

"Our Strength Is Not for Hurting" image provided by and reprinted with the permission of Men Can Stop Rape, Inc. (c) 2006 Men Can Stop Rape, Inc. Photography by Lotte Hansen.

Chapter 2

Excerpt from "The Woman" by Práxedis Guerrero, translated by Maria Massolo, found in *Against the Tide: Pro-Feminist Men in the United States, 1776-1990, A Documentary History,* edited by Michael S. Kimmel and Thomas E. Mosmiller. (c) 1992 by Michael Kimmel and Thomas Mosmiller. Reprinted by permission of Beacon, Boston.

"The Company of Men in the Procession" suffrage parade image was originally printed in New York City on May 6, 1911, and was provided by the Rare Book & Special Collections Division, Library of Congress.

"'Pregnant Men' at Birth Control Campaign, England 1972" image provided by and reprinted with the permission of Corbis. (c) Tim Graham/Hulton-Deutsch Collection/ CORBIS.

Excerpt from "Why I Stopped Trying to Be a Real Man" by John Stoltenberg. (c) John Stoltenberg. Reprinted by permission of the author. Available online at http://web .archive.org/web/20070402172337/http://www.feminista.com/archives/v1n2/ stoltenberg.html.

Chapter 3

Excerpt from "The Aggressive Egg," by David H. Freedman, published online June 1, 1992, in *Discover* magazine. (c) 1992 David H. Freedman. Reprinted by permission of the author.

"Michael Phelps" cartoon provided by and reprinted with the permission of Patrick Moberg. (c) 2008 Patrick Moberg. www.patrickmoberg.com.

Excerpt from "'Night to His Day': The Social Construction of Gender," by Judith Lorber, found in *Readings for Diversity and Social Justice: An Anthology on Racism, Antisemitism, Sexism, Heterosexism, Ableism, and Classism,* edited by Maurianne Adams, Warren J. Blumenfeld, Rosie Castañeda, et al. (c) 2000. Reprinted by permission of Routledge.

Excerpt from "That Sexe Which Prevaileth," by Anne Fausto-Sterling, found in *The Masculinity Studies Reader,* edited by Rachel Adams and David Savran. (c) 2002. Reprinted by permission of Blackwell.

Excerpt from "Masculinity as Homophobia: Fear, Shame, and Silence in the Construction of Gender Identity," by Michael S. Kimmel, found in *Readings for Diversity and Social Justice: An Anthology on Racism, Antisemitism, Sexism, Heterosexism, Ableism, and Classism,* edited by Maurianne Adams, Warren J. Blumenfeld, Rosie Castañeda, et al. (c) 2000. Reprinted by permission of Routledge.

G.I. Joe photos provided courtesy of the photographer, Betty Holmes.

"Man Box" image provided by and reprinted with the permission of Paul Kivel. (c) 1982 by Paul Kivel and the Oakland Men's Project. www.paulkivel.com.

Excerpt from "Men Growing Up to Be Boys: Madison Avenue Cultivates a Peter Pan Version of Masculinity," by Lakshmi Chaudhry, printed in *In These Times* magazine, March 17, 2006. (c) 2006. Reprinted by permission of *In These Times.*

Chapter 4

"Walk a Mile in Her Shoes" image provided by and reprinted with the permission of Associated Press. (c) AP Images/ *Laramie Daily Boomerang/* Ben Woloszyn.

This Is Not an Invitation to Rape: A Rape Prevention Campaign aimed at changing harmful attitudes toward women. Image provided by and reprinted with the permission of Peace Over Violence (formerly LACAAW).

Chapter 5

"Teach Our Sons: Real MEN Don't Hit" image was provided by and is reprinted with the permission of the photographer, Dani Meier, for the Real MEN's Project (Men Embracing Non-Violence).

Bishop Freeze "Stand Up, Speak Out" image provided by and reprinted with the permission of A Call to Men. www.acalltomen.org.

"What Men Can Do to Prevent Gender Violence," from Jackson Katz's "10 Things Men Can Do to Prevent Gender Violence," www.jacksonkatz.com.

Excerpt from "Breaking the Silence One Mile at a Time," by Grantlin Schafer, found in *Men Speak Out: Views on Gender, Sex, and Power,* edited by Shira Tarrant. (c) 2008. Reprinted by permission of Routledge.

SELECTED TITLES FROM SEAL PRESS

For more than thirty years, Seal Press has published groundbreaking books. By women. For women. Visit our website at www.sealpress.com. Check out the Seal Press blog at www.sealpress.com/blog.

Feminism and Pop Culture: Seal Studies, by Andi Zeisler. $12.95, 1-58005-237-1. Andi Zeisler, cofounder of Bitch Magazine, traces the impact of feminism on pop culture (and vice versa) from the 1940s to today.

Transgender History: Seal Studies, by Susan Stryker. $12.95, 1-58005-224-X. An introduction to transgender and queer theory from the mid–19th century through today.

Hellions: Pop Culture's Rebel Women, by Maria Raha. $15.95, 1-58005-240-1. Maria Raha, author of Cinderella's Big Score, analyzes women ranging from Marilyn Monroe to the reality TV stars of the twenty-first century in an effort to redefine the notion of female rebellion.

Women and Violence: Seal Studies, by Barrie Levy. $12.95, 1-58005-244-4. A comprehensive look at the issue of violence against women that spurs the reader to consider the impact in her life and on a global scale.

A History of U.S. Feminisms: Seal Studies, by Rory Dicker. $12.95, 1-58005-234-7. A concise introduction to feminism from the late-19th century through today.

Nobody Passes: Rejecting the Rules of Gender and Conformity, edited by Mattilda a.k.a Matt Bernstein Sycamore. $15.95, 1-58005-184-7. A timely and thought-provoking collection of essays that confronts and challenges the notion of belonging by examining the perilous intersections of identity, categorization, and community.